YOU KNOW BEST

YOU KNOW BEST

10 Rules to Elevate Your Leadership Power

Dr. Monique Dawkins

Copyright © 2023 by Monique Dawkins

"All rights reserved. No part of this publication may be reproduced in any form, or by any means, electronic or mechanical, including photocopying, recording, or any information browsing, storage, or retrieval system, without permission in writing from the publisher."

Cover Design: Boja *99Designs*

Published in the United States by Better Equipped Solutions, 10500 Little Patuxent Pkwy, P.O. Box 1356, Columbia, MD, 21044.
Better Equipped Solutions Edition 2023
First Printing

Library of Congress Cataloging-in-Publication Data
Dawkins, Monique.
You Know Best: 10 Rules to Elevate Your Leadership Power
p. cm.

ISBN (text) 979-8-9875813-0-8

ISBN (ebook) 979-8-9875813-1-5

Library of Congress Control Number: 2023902632

1- Leadership. 2- Professional Development.
3- Personal Growth. 4-Success.

"Although this publication is designed to provide accurate information in regard to the subject matter covered, the publisher and the author assume no responsibility for errors, inaccuracies, omissions, or any other inconsistencies herein. This publication is meant as a source of valuable information for the reader and the vignettes are meant to be for entertainment value and is not meant as a replacement for direct expert assistance. If such level of assistance is required, the services of a competent professional should be sought."

This book is dedicated to those who desire to have the courage to lead with integrity, intention, and purpose.

Contents

Finding My Passion   VI
Introduction   XIII

SECTION I: The Unspoken Rules   1

Chapter 1: "I got nothing."   7
Rule: Master the Art of Reading the Room

Chapter 2: "You dodged a bullet."   23
Rule: Own your Mistakes

Chapter 3: "I had plans for you."   39
Rule: Advocate for Yourself and Never Settle for Less

SECTION II: The Dirty Rules   53

Chapter 4: "This is not brain surgery!"   59
Rule: Stand Tall When Others Fall Short

Chapter 5: "My hands are tied."   75
Rule: Bad Things Can Happen to Good People

Chapter 6: "I am releasing your shackles."   89
Rule: There is No Such Thing as a Workplace Savior

SECTION III: The Rules of Thumb   101

Chapter 7: "Effective Immediately"   107
Rule: Promote your Brand

Chapter 8 : "You are already a powerful weapon and you're not even fully assembled."   121
Rule : Embody your Superpower

Chapter 9: "Do you know how impactful you are?"   133
Rule: Allow Others to Fill Your Bucket

SECTION IV: The Ultimate Rule	**147**
Chapter 10: "Remember to Breathe" *Rule: Exhale More Than You Inhale*	**153**

Afterword	167
Acknowledgements	169
About The Author	171
Learn More	173

FINDING MY PASSION

I can do anything that I aspire to do and so can you. My past experiences contribute to my worldview and have refined my approach to decision-making, critical thinking and leadership style. I have learned to welcome both opportunities and challenges that come my way and the lessons learned are shared in this book to help you to evaluate and elevate your leadership power.

My upbringing, education, and workplace knowledge and theories collectively make me who I am. I choose to be optimistic despite a career journey that has been filled with highs and lows. I consider myself a professional underdog and I have endured failure, insecurity, and hardship as a leader. My path has been detoured and rerouted many times; however, I remain determined to chase my dreams. I get through difficult situations by focusing on the big picture and choosing to silently lean in and pursue whatever I aim to accomplish. As a leader, I have personally battled workplace toxicity, systemic injustices, and poor guidance from senior leaders. I have acquired useful strategies on how to overcome unexpected situations and learned how to thrive despite power dynamics in the workplace.

My professional journey started in a similar fashion to most. After graduating from high school, I attended Howard University and attained an undergraduate degree. Despite having a bachelor's degree, my first professional position as a pharmaceutical lab assistant was lackluster and did not challenge me, and so I chose to enroll in a graduate program. I worked full time while studying for my master's degree from Pace University. Immediately after graduating, I was promoted into my first management position, a supervisory role in a large health system.

Over the decade that followed, I rose in the ranks of management. I aspired to be an executive-level leader and had no problem demonstrating my abilities and drive to get within reach of higher-level positions. Career growth was essential to my personal quest to become a senior leader, and I chose to leave organizations to advance in my profession. My long-term plans were always in the forefront of my mind as I strategically moved from organization to organization. I refused to wait for a leader or organization to see my potential. If a company did not invest in my career trajectory, I would find opportunities elsewhere.

My quest to assume increasing professional responsibility was like navigating crystal steps on a staircase with no railing. I had to be focused, strategic, and intentional about every step as I climbed the rungs from supervisor to manager to administrator, and then director. In less than eight years, I went from working as a new college graduate in my first job to working in high-profile positions with large operational oversight and people management responsibilities.

I take pleasure in the thrill of a challenging environment. While my commitment to organizations has often been limited in tenure, it has been fruitful. When I work for a company, I give them my all and work hard. I have long-standing relationships with many of my past bosses and colleagues who have worked with and for me. I remain appreciative for all the lessons learned throughout my leadership journey; they have molded me into the leader that I am today.

Because I have been privileged to lead in a variety of settings and organizations, my professional portfolio is vast and diverse. I have become familiar with the nuances of managing workforce in corporate, non-profit, private practice, unionized, and community-focused organizations. I have managed all levels of staff including entry-level employees, junior managers, independent contributors, and senior managers.

After ten years in various management positions, it dawned on me that the impact that I longed for as a leader was not within reach in the positions that I was working in. Although I had large budget responsibility, authority, and span of control, I did not feel fulfilled. I reassessed the type of impact that I wanted to have and decided that I wanted to learn more about the intersection between organizational decision-making, change management and leadership development. I decided to go back to school to study Organizational Learning and

Adult Education at Columbia University. My doctoral studies were intense, validating, and satisfying. I learned to trust the process, which I define as making the choice to accept challenges, appreciate life's mysteries and understand that I may not have control, but I can and will succeed if I choose to move forward. I spent many years researching how employees learn to cope with workplace stress and chose to write my doctoral dissertation on this topic. My research included data retrieved from interviews, focus groups, and survey responses from at least 100 individuals that suggested that workplace stress did not stem from daily responsibilities or job-associated tasks, it originated from the lack of comfort in the workplace and conflict that arose due to the inability to communicate effectively with peers, superiors, and people in positions of power.

After attaining my doctorate, I decided to take a management position focused on developing and implementing professional education and had the opportunity to partner and support hundreds of organizational leaders as they aimed to enhance collaboration and education within their teams to optimize outcomes for the larger community. It became obvious that many leaders were struggling with similar challenges; there were glaring communication gaps between internal departments and underlying tensions between employees that were rooted in the inability to manage conflict, which magnified employee stress levels and increased the potential for burnout.

I thoroughly enjoyed working in a role that allowed me to shift from problem-solving to listening, understanding, assessing, and guiding leaders to explore their version of success. It became clear that my passion was to help organizations and leaders reach their full potential through learning and development. I pursued certification as a coach from Gallup and the International Coaching Federation (ICF) because I wanted to ensure that my toolkit was diverse, as I shifted into the world of Human Resources.

In my current role, I lead learning and organizational development for a mid-sized organization and have the benefit of leaning into my passion every day as I support and cultivate learning for thousands employees. I also own a business called Better Equipped Solutions and partner with an array of organizations and individuals, including aspiring, emerging, and executive-level leaders. As a coach, my role is to partner with my clients as they discover how to get unstuck and rock it in the workplace. *You Know Best* contains the approach that I advocate with all of my coaching and consulting clients. *Your way is the best way* and when you have access to practical tools, you can design a leadership roadmap on your own terms.

INTRODUCTION

You Know Best is an invitation to curate the best version of yourself while building influence in fast-paced organizations. Management is a complex world that is often compared to trying to drink water from a fire hose. It takes dedication, determination, and business acumen to be effective. As you mature as a leader, you will find that there is much more to leadership than meets the eye. The invisible bar continues to rise, and the challenges intensify as the expectations from senior leaders become abstruse.

This book will help you increase your leadership confidence by strategically building influence and leadership power with other leaders. The principles shared focus on power dynamics, leader-to-leader interchange, and the challenges that can occur in the workplace. It can be hard to build influence in a matrix organization, where individuals report to multiple leaders. Gone are the days when you only had to focus on being accessible to your staff and aim to please your boss. It is easy to become entangled in the web of leaders and stakeholders with whom you collaborate.

∽

What if I told you that you could build influence and leadership power with other leaders in a non-stressful and organic way? Release the preconceived notion that you can read about one person's path to success and mimic their approach to achieve your desired outcome. The primary purpose of this book is to empower you by providing proven skills that can be easily adapted to increase your ability to advocate for yourself during any situation. By the end of this book, you will discover that you already have the secret sauce and that you can elevate your leadership power by engaging in reflective practices to design your own blueprint to success.

I titled this book 'You Know Best' because I believe you are in control of your leadership experience. You may not be able to control the malfunctions and hiccups that occur along the way, but you can use your power to positively influence any situation that you might face in the workplace. With 'You Know Best,' my intention is to help you reflect, process challenging career encounters, and plan to make the right choices that will benefit you professionally.

This book provides guidance for leaders seeking clarity on how to navigate ambiguous, politically driven, or messy work environments. I share ten rules that you can use to address current workplace challenges and that will help you to proactively create future opportunities. Each rule is accompanied by corresponding skills to help you navigate unforeseen roadblocks and to add to your management resources toolbox. If practically applied and used regularly, the rules, skills and reflective prompts shared will help you to feel comfortable as you boost your confidence, influence, and ultimately your power.

Definition of Leadership, Leader, and Power

Leadership is what you do. It does not define who you are. Leadership can include managing people, processes, or tasks. Working in a leadership role does not automatically equate to having control.

Leader is an inclusive term that represents all levels of management, independent contributors, and informal leaders with limited authority but responsibilities that include interaction with external and internal stakeholders.

Power is your ability to exude confidence in an intentional and impactful way that positively influences your staff, peers, or superiors.

Intended Audience

This book is written for the individual who works in a field that they enjoy and are likely proficient in functional, technical, and interpersonal abilities but want to enhance their ability to communicate clearly, confidently, and authentically when faced with conflict or unforeseen interactions with peers, superiors, or people in positions of power in the workplace.

If you've ever faced adversity, suffered a setback, felt excluded or silenced, experienced discrimination or bias based on your gender, race, or job class, or found yourself in an uncomfortable situation in the workplace, then this book is for you.

This book will benefit all leaders regardless of age, years of professional experience or industry. Adults are constantly learning and evolving despite tenure and technical ability. You are encouraged to shift your perspective and mindset by focusing on intentionally owning your power in the workplace. The rules and skills shared focus on helping you to develop personalized strategies that can be used to build influence when interacting and communicating with leaders in the workplace.

WHAT TO EXPECT

Be warned, this is not your conventional self-help book. The book is written using a blend of fiction, non-fiction, and reflective practice to provide the space for you to address your personal challenges and dilemmas and to help you plan your future course of action. If you are ready to become intentional about building your leadership brand in a way that makes you feel encouraged, empowered, and effective then buckle up, hang on tight, and get ready for the ride!

The book follows the leadership journey of a fictional character named Madison Hopeton. Her story is told through a series of *vignettes* that are fictional accounts of real events that have happened in the workplace. These are meant to both educate and entertain you. The *rules* and *skills* at the end of each chapter are corresponding best practices recommended for you as you consider how you want to be seen in the workplace. Lastly, the *reflective prompts* are meant to evoke deep thought and provide space to unpack your intentions as a leader. This learning experience can encourage and support you as you make choices that are uplifting, genuine, and justified in all aspects of your life.

My hope is that you walk away feeling inspired and ready to survive and thrive in the world of leadership. *You Know Best* provides a clear and practical guideline that can be applied to reinforce authentic leadership. Side effects may include a surge in confidence and the ability to feel good about leading in the workplace on your own terms. Enjoy!

SECTION I
THE UNSPOKEN RULES

Many assumptions are made in the workplace. Starting with the basics, you are expected to know how to do your job. Professional performance includes being able to proficiently execute all the tasks and competencies listed in your job description. You were hired because you successfully articulated past accomplishments that indicated that you would be a good fit for the job in question. Alternatively, you may have been able to demonstrate the promise of performing in the described role based on your past experience. Once you are hired into a position, it is automatically assumed that you are working hard to satisfy all of the requirements. To remain effective as a leader, you will need to establish relationships with key stakeholders and learn how to collaborate in an effort to successfully partner and engage with others; it is important that you commit and do this with purpose.

Leadership is an ever-changing environment with limited instruction guides, myriad competing priorities, and hefty expectations. Some leaders have people who report to them. Others may be independent contributors to the organization and manage projects or programs. All leaders (whether or not they lead others in the workplace) hold a lot of responsibilities and constantly interact with a multitude of people in their organizations.

Emerging leaders, or those newer in their positions, often focus on asserting their authority and building relationships with their direct reports. Most of their time is spent in the "storming, forming, and norming" process with teams and accomplishing tasks set by their boss. Mature leaders expand their focus beyond team dynamics and process implementation. They begin to understand the importance of establishing a distinguished reputation with all levels of management inclusive of 'informal' leaders and external stakeholders. Expert leaders realize that building influence is power and are deliberate about establishing partnerships, gaining buy-in prior to making decisions while fostering key relationships in the workplace.

Consider everything you experience in the workplace as a tangible learning moment. Learning moments are personal and meaningful based on your needs and aspirations in a specific period of time. You can sit in the same room as a peer and go through the same situation. While they might walk away with no value-added, you might have just experienced an invaluable lesson. The goal is not to compare situations or experiences but to focus on your needs to better yourself as a leader.

Learn to Master the Unspoken Rules

In the upcoming chapters, prepare to learn about the facets of leadership that are often assumed yet never clearly explained to leaders. The rules in this section address the prevalence of ambiguity amongst all levels of leadership. The skills listed below are discussed in detail in the upcoming chapters. These techniques are designed to help you learn to be agile and strategic in the workplace.

Rule 1: MASTER THE ART OF READING THE ROOM

SKILLS
Know your audience.
Understand the difference between curiosity and cluelessness.
Think before you speak.

Rule 2: OWN YOUR MISTAKES

SKILLS
Acknowledge your role.
Make a commitment.
Check your ego.

Rule 3: ADVOCATE FOR YOURSELF AND NEVER SETTLE FOR LESS

SKILLS
Say it out loud.
Be calculated.
Redefine the idea of loyalty.

"I got nothing."
MASTER THE ART OF READING THE ROOM

The room was so silent that you could hear a pin drop. A sea of leaders sat on meticulously placed folding chairs. Nerves and tension filled the air. The faces represented hues of white, brown and all shades in-between. Regardless of gender, their expressions were stern and focused, as if it were game day on the football field.

Anxiety was at a peak for Madison Hopeton and Shaina Cole as they nervously reviewed the presentation that they would be delivering to the leadership council in mere moments. Madison and Shaina were supervisors who worked together in the same department of a large for-profit organization. They had started their jobs a few weeks apart, and this was the first time they would present the financials for their business service line in front of the entire management team.

The Chief Financial Officer Dan Kennedy led this monthly mandatory leadership meeting, held in the largest auditorium on campus, the only room that could house the 500 leaders. Dan was the embodiment of frank and abrasive. He did not understand what the word, fluff, meant; he was always 100 percent business.

"Dan always seems so stressed out," Madison whispered to Shaina who was deep in thought as she practiced for their presentation.

At last, the "pin dropped"—all anyone in the room could hear was the strong, measured steps that Dan took as he approached the front of the auditorium. His pace was quick and filled with purpose, signaling that he had places to be because time was money. They all knew that he did not play about money. All heads raised and spines straightened, as the leaders fumbled to ensure that their phones were silenced.

Dan tolerated neither phone interruptions nor late arrivals. He had made an example out of many individuals for perpetrating these unspeakable acts. Although anyone could fall prey to one of these mistakes, Dan had made it clear. If you chose to disrespect his meeting, you were dead to him. The fear ran so deep that the one time Madison was two minutes late due to a faulty elevator, instead of sneaking into the back of the room she stayed outside, texting Shaina the information she would need to ensure the department was represented well.

Madison and many other newbies in the room had learned six months ago just how vicious Dan could be when he was tested. Another employee, Paul Johnson, had arrived five minutes late to a now infamous meeting and attempted to slip into a vacant chair in the back of the room.

"Who do you think you are?" Dan's voice had boomed from the podium. He had been greeting the entire leadership team and in no time flat, his pleasant tone shifted from authoritative and knowledgeable to that of the Terminator. Paul had not responded, hoping that Dan was not speaking to him. But Dan had a wireless microphone, and he had started making his way to the back of the room.

"Who do you think you are?" Dan asked again, now just a few feet away from Paul.

Paul's face was riddled with guilt, shame, and fear—despite his leadership role as director of operations. "Dan, my apologies," Paul quietly murmured hoping this would end the interrogation.

All eyes in the room were fixed on Paul. Everyone had now shifted, twisting their torsos to watch the show. Dan walked right up to Paul, leaning in close to read his name badge.

"Paul Johnson from Marketing, is it?" Dan pushed his glasses toward the tip of his nose as he read the badge on Paul's suit jacket lapel.

"Yes." Paul's voice was full of exasperation.

"Come with me." Dan ordered as he spun around and headed to the front of the room.

The request to follow was not optional. Understanding this, Paul stood up like a nine year old who had been caught stealing, and slowly walked behind Dan.

Everyone sat in astonishment, looking back and forth at each other, eyes wide and jaws open, as Dan led Paul up to the front of the room. Dan ushered Paul onto the podium.

"So, this is Paul everyone. Paul thinks it is okay to come to my meeting whenever he feels like it and so that must mean he wants to present the KPI metrics and financial updates for his department to the group." Dan's speech was clipped. He pursed his lips and took a seat. Taking his time, he crossed his legs and sat comfortably in his chair like a mob boss.

"I am not prepared to give a presentation," Paul replied. He spoke so quietly that folks in the back of the room could barely hear his response.

"So, you walk in here late, but you don't have information to share?" Dan continued to jab at Paul.

Paul shifted his weight from leg to leg, looking as if he might pass out at any moment. Dan glanced at his watch, back at Paul, and then stood up. "Clearly you are not prepared to do anything except disrupt the meeting today," he said. "You are excused."

Paul did not need a second request to leave the stage. He practically flew back to his seat. The lesson was set in stone for all leaders across the organization. Never ever come late to a Dan Kennedy meeting.

"Madison!" Shaina hissed with urgency. "We're up next. Are you ready?"

Shaina's leg softly bounced up and down, as she checked the time on her cellphone. Her cream-colored skin looked rosy, and her blond hair was in a messy bun on top of her head. She complemented her casual hairstyle with gold-stud earrings. Black-rimmed glasses and pale pink lipstick completed her look.

Madison glanced over with a casual grin, which immediately helped Shaina relax. She nodded her head and shifted her glance back to Dan as he concluded the quarterly welcome.

Madison tucked her deep-brown hair behind her ears and reached into her purse to retouch her mocha lip-gloss. Her caramel complexion was complemented with flawless makeup and her natural, afro-textured hair sprouted blonde and brown coils all over her head. She looked like she was ready to sit down in the anchor chair at WPIX news.

Madison felt more than ready. She had worked late

all week reviewing the information for the presentation. Less than an hour ago, she had a meeting with their boss, Tim Brooks, at his suggestion, to go over the materials one final time and bring him up to speed. Tim was the Director of their department. Typically the head of the team presented in these meetings. But in the previous week's team huddle, he had decided prior that it would be good practice for Madison and Shaina to take the lead in the presentation. He assured them that he would be right by their side to back them up as needed.

When their department was called, Madison and Shaina rose from their seats in unison. They walked to the front of the room and Shaina grabbed the wireless remote used to advance the slides and joined Madison on the stage. Madison noticed that Tim was not joining them as planned. She attempted to mask the quizzical look on her face as she tried to make eye contact with him from the stage. Tim simply gave a soft nod and supportive smile from his seat. Shaina peered with wide eyes at Madison, silently asking for direction, and Madison calmly gave a soft nod indicating that they should start the presentation.

They spent the next six minutes providing highlights of their financials and prospective growth opportunities for the upcoming quarter. As rehearsed, they did their best to address all potential questions in advance, hoping that Dan would have no follow-up questions and certainly no concerns. Once they finished, they stood quietly waiting for the verdict from Dan. He sat in a stoic fashion in his self-assigned seat in the front row. He looked at the handout that they'd provided, which summarized their findings. "Where is Tim?" Dan blurted. He looked to both his left and right.

Shaina fiddled with the remote, and Madison had a weird plastic smile plastered on her face as if she was participating in a photo shoot.

"I'm here, Dan," Tim said. His voice seemed to emerge from the right side of the auditorium. He sat close to the front of the room in the third row in an aisle seat. He sat with his legs crossed, slightly slouched in his chair with his iced coffee in hand as he responded.

"What is your theory on why your department did not achieve the forecasted budget last month?" Dan barked. Madison and Shaina stood stock-still, like an incomplete version of Charlie's Angels, as they waited for Tim to respond.

Tim casually took a sip of his coffee and appeared to hunker down in his seat. There was an awkward silence while everyone waited for his response. He took his time, as if he were not being asked a critical question from *the* Dan Kennedy in front of hundreds of leaders with his dignity on the line. "I got nothing," he casually responded.

"Excuse me?" Dan asked incredulously.

"I got nothing," Tim said again. "Madison…what do you think?" Without missing a beat, he pitched the hot potato right back to the women on the stage. Dan shifted his attention back to Madison and Shaina.

Madison was shocked. Although she had just reviewed this with Tim, she could not recall the reason for the variance in the budget. She squinted her eyes in Tim's direction hoping that he would take the hint and assist with answering Dan's query. Tim met her eyes with a shoulder shrug indicating that he had nothing to add.

Before she could make an excuse, Shaina jumped in, providing the information that Dan had requested. Her answer appeared to satisfy him because moments later they were dismissed from the stage. They went back to their seats feeling relieved that their grilling session was over. The meeting ended 90 minutes later, and the room emptied in a matter of seconds.

The hallway outside of the auditorium was filled to capacity. It was busy and loud with some people casually making small talk, relieved to be out of the pressure-filled meeting, and others hurrying to their next meeting. Tim walked up to Madison and Shaina with a big smile.

"Nice job, ladies!" Tim grinned, looking genuinely pleased.

Both ladies exchanged quick glances and nodded. Madison shifted her eyes to her cellphone to check the time and to avoid direct eye contact with Tim. She was not gifted with a poker face and did not want him to sense her irritation.

"Madison, that was a good exercise for you up there today. When Dan asks you something you don't know, just be honest and let him know. We can always send the information to him later."

Tim did not wait for a response as his phone chirped. He glanced down to check the message as Madison rolled her eyes in frustration.

"I have to run, but again, you both did great! See you at the 3 pm meeting later this afternoon!" Tim barely looked up from his phone as he turned toward the elevators and headed back to his office. As he walked away, Madison tilted her head and looked at Shaina in disbelief.

"Let's do lunch," Shaina said.

They walked two blocks before Madison finally broke the silence. "I appreciate you for having my back in there." Madison's voice was soft as she spoke.

"Not a problem, my friend. We have to support each other." Shaina replied optimistically as they walked up Fifth Avenue toward their favorite Mexican spot.

Madison shook her head incredulously, "We couldn't make this up!" Shaina nodded her head in agreement and stopped walking.

"Madison, why do you think your boss threw you under the bus in there?" Shaina queried jokingly.

Madison slowed her pace down a bit. Her nose flared as she paused, smirked, and responded sarcastically, "I got nothing!" Her voice mimicked Tim's monotone and calm disposition. They looked at each other and broke into gut-busting laughter that instantly made everything better.

POST-CHAPTER REFLECTION

* What stood out for you in this story?
* How does it make you feel when you witness off-putting or abrasive behavior from a person in a position of power?
* What is Worse: A boss who fails to support you during a group presentation *or* a boss who seems oblivious to tense situations?

THE BOTTOM LINE

Reading the room is an art and not a science. This is the class that is not offered in undergraduate or graduate school, yet the ability to skillfully read the room is often an essential competency that either validates or invalidates a leader's credibility. The ability to read the room is not relegated to a particular position in the workplace. It is a requirement of effective leadership and can enhance the tact, style, and influence that a leader has in an organization.

WHAT YOU NEED TO KNOW

Leaders are always figurately on a stage. Remember that all interactions, particularly those with other leaders, are important and you should always modify your approach based on the audience.

The following skills can help you demonstrate the ability to read the room:

SKILLS	
	Know your audience.
	Understand the difference between curiosity and cluelessness.
	Think before you speak.

The reflective prompts shared throughout this chapter are designed to help you consider your purpose and expectations that you are hoping to achieve as you intentionally utilize these techniques.

KNOW YOUR AUDIENCE. Consider the appropriateness of information shared at any given time in the workplace. You interact and speak with many people at work. Some colleagues may work in more senior roles, while others may be in junior positions. It is important to understand the type of information that everyone expects or requires from you so that you can deliver an appropriate message. As a leader, you must use your discretion to understand what information to share and with whom. Depending on your role, you might make different determinations on what information is appropriate to share with others in the workplace. As you prepare to have important conversations, ask yourself guiding questions to gauge the appropriateness and necessity of the information that you intend to share.

* What is your process for deciding what information needs to be shared with others in the workplace?
* After defining the content of the message, what steps do you take to tailor the information based on the audience?
* How do you know if your message was received positively or negatively?

UNDERSTAND THE DIFFERENCE BETWEEN CURIOSITY AND CLUELESSNESS. Leaders are encouraged to be curious. The strongest leaders are often those that choose to ask the tough questions and constantly encourage their teams to share information. Curiosity in the workplace should be used as a strategic tool and not be aimless. In management positions or leadership roles, people listen to what you say just as intently as they listen for what you do not say. They silently take notice of the information that you share and of the questions that you ask aloud. Many presume that leaders are purposeful in their line of questioning. People believe leaders are collecting key information, validating a theory, or attempting to disprove a myth that may be circulating. The understanding is that the leader's questions are being asked from a place of intention and not triviality. It is important to take note of your audience when you are asking questions. Based on your role and your needs, make sure that your comments stem from a place of curiosity and not a place of cluelessness to avoid losing legitimacy as it relates to your competency and abilities.

* How do you decipher the difference between an aimless conversation as opposed to one that is mutually beneficial?
* How do you decide who you can be 'clueless' in front of as opposed to polished and curious?
* What can you do to become more intentional about your line of questioning when interacting with others in formal workplace settings?

THINK BEFORE YOU SPEAK. Some leaders—like Dan as described in the vignette—choose to use their position as a shield to protect themselves from the need to communicate with tact. Body language and tone are always being monitored by others in your organization. What you choose to say or not say in response to questions you are asked in an open forum is important and should not be taken lightly. While presenting yourself as human and incorporating genuine traits of your personality at work, it is also important to present yourself as a subject matter expert. Always represent yourself well because your ability to articulate clearly and logically can elevate your professional reputation. Think about what information your peers and senior leaders may require from you before you have critical conversations. Be prepared and ask the right questions to obtain the information that you need and respond concisely.

* Do you regularly tend to ask questions or provide information at work?
* How do you think people perceive you as a leader at work?
* What do you want people to take away from every interaction with you as a leader?

FINAL REFLECTION

* On a scale of 1 (poor) to 10 (superpower), how would you rate your ability to read the room?
* What challenges have you faced in your past attempts to read the room?
* What opportunities may be present for you to consider after reading this chapter?

IN SUMMARY

MASTER THE ART OF READING THE ROOM by ensuring that you *know your audience*, purposefully *differentiate between curiosity and cluelessness*, and *think before you speak*. This will highlight your ability to communicate in a clear, concise, and impactful manner.

"*You dodged a bullet.*"
OWN YOUR MISTAKES

A year had flown by in the blink of an eye. Madison had been promoted to a practice manager position within the same organization. Much had changed in such a short amount of time, but she was grateful for the opportunity to learn and add value to the organization in a meaningful way. The transition into her new role had been painless. She appreciated that she still shared an office with Shaina, her work bestie and partner in crime. She loved having someone to vent to and bounce crazy ideas off of in the heat of the moment.

As Madison sat at her desk, looking at her calendar, she felt overwhelmed. *Damn, today is going to be super busy.* She had back-to-back meetings, including five candidate interviews. She was actively hiring for a project coordinator position and hoped to find a suitable candidate quickly so that she could end this exhaustive search. She got up from her desk, grabbed her favorite mug, and headed to the kitchen to get a coffee refill. Although she was already on her second cup, she felt drained just thinking about the day ahead. She filled her mug and headed toward the conference room for the first meeting of the day. Three hours and three meetings later, she was starving but unfortunately, she had another interview that started five minutes ago. She ran into her office, took two bites of a sandwich that she had brought from home, swiftly exited, and hurried toward the first floor conference room.

As she approached the glass door, she saw a young woman probably in her early twenties-waiting in the conference room. Madison put on her game face, opened the door, and walked in.

"Hi, I am Madison, are you Janet?" She flashed a warm smile and extended a hand to greet the candidate. Janet quickly rose to her feet and smiled revealing deep dimples and greeted Madison with a firm handshake. Madison took a seat at the head of the table, in a chair adjacent to the candidate.

"Yes, I am Janet. It's so nice to meet you, Madison. This place is beautiful," Janet said. Her words were jumbled and came out too fast. Madison smiled.

Apparently, she wasn't the only one who'd had too much coffee.

"Do you have a copy of your resume?" Madison asked. She always had a copy with her just in case, so this was a test to see how prepared the candidate was for the job interview.

"Of course," Janet chirped. She handed over a perfectly assembled resume, printed on thick resume paper. Madison was impressed; most people used cheap copier paper. She skimmed the neatly formatted document.

"Tell me about yourself?" Madison said. Relaxing her shoulders, she leaned forward in her chair, and waited for the response.

Janet smiled and replied with a perfect elevator pitch that included her background, interest in the role, and squeezed in a few highlights about why she would be a good fit—all in 90 seconds.

'*Impressive*,' Madison thought. For the next 30 minutes, Janet answered every question impeccably and seemed qualified for the role. Madison stood up after the last question, shook Janet's hand, and thanked her for her time.

She checked her work calendar on her phone and moved on to the next meeting. She finally finished her sandwich around 3:00 pm, and concluded all her meetings and scheduled interviews by 5:30. She was exhausted. Although she had a report due in the morning, Madison knew it was time to head home and regroup.

The next day, when she arrived at her office, there was a card on her desk. "Where did this come from?" she asked.

"No clue," Shaina answered from her desk. She looked as stressed as Madison had felt the day before and didn't even look up from her computer. Madison put her lunch in the mini fridge, dropped her workbag on the table next to her modest desk, turned on her computer, and picked up the small blue postcard. She turned it over to see a handwritten note from Janet.

"Dag, she moves fast," Madison said. "This is from the candidate I interviewed yesterday. She must really want this job. Not too many people send handwritten thank-you notes after interviews anymore." Even a thank you email was considered going above and beyond in this fast-paced hiring process.

"Are you considering her for the position?" Shaina asked.

Madison was already distracted by the 50 emails that she'd received overnight. *Do people sleep anymore, or do they just work 24-hours-day?* She spent a few minutes addressing emails before responding to Shaina.

"I think I'm going to hire her. We really need to fill the position."

"Oh wow! You must have really liked her," Shaina said.

"Ehh, she was okay, but I'm really overwhelmed. Out of the interviews I've done so far, Janet seems to be the most qualified," Madison said, thinking out loud more than actually responding to Shania's question.

"I understand. Have you checked her references or introduced her to anyone on the team to get an additional opinion?"

Shaina was asking good questions, but she was getting on Madison's nerves. She did typically include Shaina in the interview process since they were peers in the department, but time was of the essence. Janet had gone the extra mile with this handwritten note. Madison also typically held a second round of interviews, but she just did not have the time. She was already stretched thin.

Madison grabbed her mug as she looked at her calendar and groaned. The day was just as busy as the day before. Nine hours went by in a blur. After the most bizarre interview at the end of the day with a gentleman who kept referring to himself in the third person, Madison decided that she would extend an offer to Janet. She was tired of interviewing and was even more convinced that Janet would do a respectable job in the role.

Three weeks later, Janet arrived for her first day of work as a project coordinator. She was a quick learner and eager to help. Everything was going well until it wasn't. Six weeks in, things started to crack. Janet refused to send emails or even to use a sticky note to leave messages. She often interrupted meetings inappropriately. She overbooked Madison's calendar, ignoring the block time that Madison reserved to get work done. Madison started to resent Janet and didn't want to work with her at all.

Before long, Janet became the office gossip and began sharing scandalous chatter, constantly missing Madison's polite cues of disinterest. Janet crossed the final line when she failed to alert Madison that an important client, who she'd been waiting to speak with for weeks, had returned her call. Instead of interrupting Madison in a meeting—as she had previously done for irrelevant calls—Janet told the caller that Madison was busy, even though a big deadline hinged on speaking with the client.

"Oh Madison, Mr. Miller called, and I told him you would call him back," Janet said casually.

Madison stopped in her tracks. "What?" She was acutely aware that her tone was not as measured as it normally was, but she was already feeling the stress, having attended a particularly infuriating meeting that was way too long and could have been a memo instead.

"I know you said I should stop interrupting your meetings," Janet said, her eyes wide.

"No! I asked you to use discretion when you interrupt my meetings, and you knew I was waiting for his call." Madison spun on her heels and rushed into her office. Her veins pulsed. She sat and grabbed the phone to call her client. The phone rang twice and then went voicemail. The office was closed for the holiday. Madison hit the prompt to leave a personal voice mail for Mr. Miller and discovered that that he would be out on vacation for the next two weeks.

"Damn it!" Madison said. She rubbed her temples. *Janet needs to go*, she thought to herself. Shoving her outstanding work into her bag, she prepared to leave for the day. Shania's advice on checking references and getting a second opinion came to mind and her head started to throb. Maybe Janet's departure from her last job had not been voluntary. Madison resolved to speak with someone from Human Resources (HR)on Tuesday when she returned from the holiday.

Early on Tuesday, Madison sat in the HR office venting to Marcus, her HR representative. He listened to Madison's concerns and nodded his head, a supportive look on his face.

"She is not a good fit, and I want her gone. I plan to let her go today," Madison said.

Marcus' expression went from supportive to alarmed. "Oh no, Madison. I am sorry you are having these concerns, but I don't think we want the risk of firing her if you don't have a firm reason to do so."

This was not what Madison expected to hear. She rolled her eyes and stood to her feet in a defensive stance.

Marcus calmly looked up at Madison from his chair and waited for the next round of venting. This was typical in Human Resources. Manager hires employee, manager does not screen and vet employee, employee seems great at first but ends up being mediocre, and manager wants to fire employee with no solid grounds.

"She is not a good fit," Madison said. She began to recite the facts that validated her request to terminate Janet.

Marcus stared blankly and remained unmoved. After about an hour, Madison realized that the discussion was going nowhere, and she was almost late for her next meeting.

"Why don't you speak to Janet and share your concerns. Also, remember to document every conversation as a backup," Marcus said, standing up to walk Madison to the door.

As she waited for the elevator, Madison looked at the calendar on her cell phone. She pressed the elevator button call button again, beginning to worry that she would be miss the start of her next meeting. The elevator finally arrived. As the grey doors slid open, out walked Janet.

"Good morning, Madison." Janet said with a polite smile as she passed by and walked into the Human Resources office.

What the hell is she doing in there? Madison thought, awkwardly returning the greeting. She stepped into the elevator, hurriedly pressing her floor.

Madison bounced from meeting to meeting until she got a reprieve around 2:30 that afternoon. She hadn't checked her email in hours. Depleted from the busy day, she grabbed her sandwich from the fridge and sat down to catch up on email. She scrolled through emails and saw she had a message from Marcus.

Before she could click open the message, the phone rang. "Hello," Madison answered.

"I have great news," Marcus said.

Madison sat up in her chair, alert and at full attention.

"I can fire Janet?" Madison asked impatiently.

"No."

Madison rolled her eyes and slouched in her chair.

"Well, what is the 'great' news then?"

"The good news is that Janet resigned today, stating it was for personal reasons," Marcus said. "You dodged a bullet."

Madison closed her eyes and took a deep breath. "This is the best news that I've heard all day," she said.

They spoke for a few more minutes before concluding

the call. Madison sat at her desk and thought about how dreadful the last few months had been because of her overzealous decision to hire Janet. *I won't make that mistake again.* She gathered her things and decided to end the day early as an act of celebration.

POST-CHAPTER REFLECTION

* What stood out for you in this story?
* How does it make you feel when you make a poor choice that comes back to haunt you?
* What is Worse: Hiring the wrong person in haste *or* knowing that you could have avoided the mistake by incorporating feedback from a peer?

THE BOTTOM LINE

Every leader has, at times, made a decision that turned out to be less than ideal. Among the choices, it may have seemed like the best option at the time. As a leader, you will inevitably make a poor decision that you regret. Mistakes are to be expected. While it does not feel good when you are resolving a situation that could have been avoided, don't be too hard on yourself. Take advantage of learning from the mishap as opposed to punishing yourself for not making the ideal choice.

WHAT YOU NEED TO KNOW

> Leaders make mistakes. There is something that can be learned from all interactions in the workplace, especially those that we regret.

The following skills can help you as you explore your role in owning a mistake and developing a path forward:

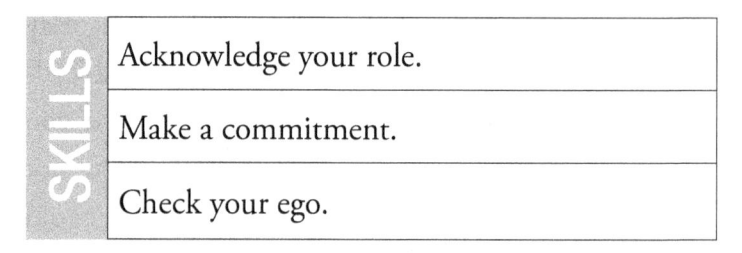

SKILLS
Acknowledge your role.
Make a commitment.
Check your ego.

The reflective prompts shared throughout this chapter are designed to help you consider your purpose and expectations that you are hoping to achieve as you intentionally utilize these techniques.

ACKNOWLEDGE YOUR ROLE. Take a moment and accept your part in the situation, circumstance, or challenge. Reflect on why you have faced challenges in the past. Perhaps political layers in the organization blocked you from making the right choice? Or an overwhelming workload prevented you from proper vetting or preparation. It is often easy to play the blame game to justify why a mistake was made. Allow yourself a brief pity party where you point the finger at everyone else who could have helped you avoid the mistake, and then shift the focus to what you can do!

* How do you hold yourself accountable after making an unfavorable decision?

* What value can a mentor or trusted advisor play in processing the current situation and planning a path forward?
* What limits you from being successful during challenging times?

MAKE A COMMITMENT. Rise to the occasion and modify your leadership approach to improve your future decision-making processes. Pressure and lack of time are constants that can increase the probability of being put in a situation that might lead to a poor choice. After you have acknowledged your role and contribution to the challenge or situation, it is time to move forward with intention. Commit to doing something differently to avoid repeating the cycle.

* What is your preferred pace when making decisions?
* How do you feel when you are pressured to make tough decisions?
* How can you ensure that your future actions are proactive and not reactive?

CHECK YOUR EGO. Make a pledge to yourself. Dig beneath the surface and allow yourself to truly learn from this challenge. You may have identified *why* you have faced this circumstance and hopefully have taken the time to process *how* you will move forward by committing to alternative actions and approaches. Yet, despite regular self-reflection and problem-solving, you may be glossing over glaring aspects of your personality or leadership style that have put you in this predicament. Put your ego to the side and realize that you are not guilt free. You have the opportunity to learn through insights and to modify your approach to managing challenges.

- What is your preferred decision-making style at work?
- Why is it important to have others weigh in on something that is within your purview of authority?
- What is it about your decision-making approach that could use some fine-tuning?

FINAL REFLECTION

* On a scale of 1 (poor) to 10 (superpower), how would you rate your willingness to own your mistakes?
* What challenges have you faced in your past attempts to own your mistakes?
* What opportunities may be present for you to consider after reading this chapter?

IN SUMMARY

OWN YOUR MISTAKES. Choose to *acknowledge your role*, *make a commitment*, and *check your ego*. This will ensure you are maturing as a leader and learning from all workplace mishaps.

"*I had plans for you.*"
ADVOCATE FOR YOURSELF AND NEVER SETTLE

Madison sat at her desk fidgeting uncomfortably because she had successfully spent the entire day avoiding the one task that had to be completed before the end of the day. She picked up her phone to see if there were any urgent messages and had no new notifications because she had just looked at the screen ten seconds ago. *Get yourself together girl and be the boss chick that you are.* Procrastinating any longer would not be fruitful. Madison took a deep breath, grabbed her notebook, and before she could change her mind, walked with a determined pace toward her boss's office.

Keith was the Senior Director to whom she had reported to for the past two years in her position as a

Business Manager. She loved working with Keith. In her four-year management tenure, he was her favorite boss by far. He was super smart and not threatened by the talents of the team that reported to him, which had not been her experience in the past. He always encouraged her to take the lead and welcomed radical thoughts and innovation. He was great at supporting her ideas publicly in meetings and had been a much-needed mentor, helping her make an easy transition into the new organization.

She took three deep breaths to quell her nerves and knocked on Keith's door. Through the glass of his office door, Madison could see Keith at his desk typing. He looked up when she knocked.

"Yep," he called without turning from his desk.

Madison pushed the door open and stuck her head in. "Hey Keith, is now a good time?" She was hoping that he would ask her to come back another time.

"What a pleasant surprise," Keith said. He glanced to the side but continued to type. "Of course. Just give me one second."

Madison walked in and took a seat. Settling into the plush leather chair, she watched Keith as he appeared to ponder his response, and then furiously continued typing away, lost in whatever situation he was handling at the moment. He was the type of manager who wrote long responses to simple emails.

Madison thought about the reason she was here. Today she would formally resign from her position. Keith wouldn't be pleased, and she worried that he would take it personally. This was not the first time she had been down this path. Thirteen months earlier, she had almost resigned despite receiving a great performance review. At the time, she had appreciated Keith's insightful and supportive comments during the meeting, but she was disappointed that he had not offered her a promotion.

Keith had created a new director-level position for the company that would have been a challenging and exciting new role for Madison. She had not formally applied, but she secretly hoped he would consider her and that they would discuss the opportunity during her performance evaluation. She patiently waited during the discussion for him to bring up the position. He had not and so, at the end of the meeting, she casually asked him some questions about the new role. She was hoping he would have an epiphany and realize that she was interested. That did not happen. Instead, he told her that she would receive the maximum merit increase for her "exceeds expectations" rating. He'd all but patted her on the shoulder as he ushered her out of the office.

Madison was so disappointed. She shared her devastation with her fiancé, Nathan. He consoled her and told her that she had two choices, either revisit her professional development plans with her boss or move on and find another job that would meet her needs. She chose the latter and spent a substantial portion of the next week job hunting. She applied to countless jobs and quickly received calls from recruiters offering her interviews. Three weeks from the date of her performance evaluation with Keith, she accepted an offer for a more advanced position with additional responsibilities and a $20,000 salary increase.

She was excited about her new job but anxious that Keith would be disappointed about her departure. She stormed into his office, the first thing on a Monday morning, and attacked him before he could even drink his first cup of coffee. He looked so surprised to see Madison in the office before 8 am, and offered her a seat to hear what was so urgent that she had not even stopped at her desk to put down her coat and purse before coming to see him. She blurted out the news of her resignation and stared at him from the door of his office. He insisted that she have a seat and calmly urged her to share what led her to this rash decision.

Before he allowed her to speak, he took a few sips of his coffee and turned his desk chair to face her, leaning forward. "What can I do to keep you here?" he asked.

Madison was caught off guard. She had resigned from other jobs in the past, but this was harder because she enjoyed working with Keith.

"I....I....I am ready for more." Madison struggled to put her reasoning into words. She wanted to assert herself without offending Keith.

"I agree." His response was quick.

Madison felt conflicted and blinked back tears. She knew that he was in the middle of interviewing final candidates for the new position that she believed should have been offered to her. "I work hard and deserve more," Madison said quietly.

"You are absolutely right, Madison. I thought you knew how much I value you from all the praise I put in your performance evaluation a few weeks ago." He paused and looked directly into her eyes. Keith took a few more sips of coffee, then put his mug down. "How much more money will you be making in your new position?"

Madison had been in Keith's office for less than five minutes. Exhaustion overwhelmed her. She expected him to be dissatisfied but had not expected him to try and retain her in her role.

"Twenty thousand." Her voice was barely above a whisper.

Keith stood up from his chair and paced a few steps. Other than the sound of his feet on the carpet, the room was quiet. Madison heard the sounds of the office coming to life outside of Keith's door. The administrative staff were starting to arrive and could be heard chit-chatting in the distance. Madison resisted the urge to get up and run out of the office, sitting still in her seat, barely breathing.

"Madison." Keith said her name for a second time.

"I am sorry, you were saying?" she asked.

"I was saying that I can offer you a $10,000 raise, starting today. I want you to stay on the team, we need you."

Madison's mouth dropped open in surprise.

Keith continued. "You're a valuable member of the team, and we need your expertise." His smile was supportive as he stood with his hand extended.

Madison felt as if she just lost a 12-round heavy weight battle. She accepted his handshake and with that, his terms.

She blinked a few times to snap out of replaying the old scenario and focus on the present moment. Keith was still typing away. Now 13 months later, despite the increase in her paycheck, she had not been challenged. She felt as if she was stuck on autopilot. Keith had hired Ivan in the director role he'd created. Madison had partnered with Ivan frequently over the past few months and wanted the autonomy and scope of his role for herself.

Recently she had been contacted by a recruiter and had gone through the screening process for a new position. She'd been impressed by the leaders and the scope of work that she would be responsible in the job. The role was more dynamic, and included a $10,000 raise, putting her in the salary on par with that of the previous job she that had passed up last year.

Keith turned from his computer, finally finished. "I am sorry Madison. I get so annoyed when I get these inflammatory emails from our legal team. I needed to fill them in on some pertinent information. Sorry to keep you waiting." As he spoke, his shoulders relaxed, and he settled into his chair.

Madison looked Keith in the eyes and said, "I am sorry to do this Keith, but I have been offered a really great opportunity."

Keith tried to interject, but Madison held up her hand to interrupt him before she could lose her nerve. "I really and I do mean *really* appreciate all that I have learned from you over these past few years, but I feel like I have reached the ceiling at this company." She held her hand out with the perfunctory letter that had her resignation details.

"Damn," Keith blurted as he took the white envelope from her hand. He simply placed the envelope on his desk and stood, wishing her the best of luck.

As he walked her to the door, he placed a hand on her shoulder and said, "I had plans for you" and turned to walk back in his chair.

Keith's response caught her off guard and she pondered the meaning behind his words. How long had Keith had these plans for her and when he was planning to unveil them? Madison felt confident in her decision this time around and did not regret taking advantage of an upward promotion. She was finally choosing herself and it felt good.

POST-CHAPTER REFLECTION

* What stood out for you in this story?
* How would you feel if you were overlooked for an internal advancement opportunity?
* What is worse: Having a boss who is unaware of your career aspirations *or* not having an established relationship with your boss that encourages you to share your career goals?

THE BOTTOM LINE

Gaining experience in the field can be invigorating and can begin to shape your future interests. However, the combination of ambiguity and assumptions can lead to disappointment for both the leader and organization. Once you begin to imagine a growth trajectory of choice, don't be afraid to discuss your interests and make decisions that serve you.

WHAT YOU NEED TO KNOW

> Leaders always identify and emphasize their value proposition while advocating for their ambitions in the organization. Remember that your long-term goals and career aspirations are important and should be made known in the organization.

The following skills can help you refine your path while advocating for yourself along the way.

SKILLS	
	Say it out loud.
	Be calculated.
	Redefine the idea of loyalty.

The reflective prompts shared throughout this chapter are designed to help you consider your purpose and expectations that you are hoping to achieve as you intentionally utilize these techniques

SAY IT OUT LOUD. Force your inner voice out into the universe. This requires you to use your words to do something that may feel dangerous and uncomfortable in the beginning. Speaking up and sharing your hidden interests and future goals can seem risky, but removes ambiguity for senior leaders and those who may be invested in your future with the organization. Being deliberate and clear about your career interests and coveted trajectory is a bold move. But you may be missing out on opportunities due to lack of communication. You are in charge of your future, and you hold more power than you may realize. How you speak up is important. Share your interests versus making ultimatums. Choose your words wisely and keep your tone, approach, and energy light when engaging in these types of discussions. Give yourself adequate time to formulate your thoughts before you initiate career-growth conversations in the workplace.

* What type of opportunities would satisfy you as you consider you desired career trajectory?
* What is something your boss or organization does not know about you that they should know?
* What steps can you take to regularly share your vision for growth, professional development, and or coveted workplace opportunities with your boss?

BE CALCULATED. Take appropriate risks at the right time. Growth and opportunity mean different things to different people. Professional development can be nuanced, and senior leaders' assumptions about the career aims of the individuals that report to them may be off the mark. To create alignment, there must be clarity and a plan between you and your supervisor. It is important to mention that speaking up and articulating your goals and future plans with your organization does not equate to a promise or commitment to never leave the organization. The purpose of speaking up is to ensure that all parties are clear about your aspirations. Once you have shared your interests, this gives your organization the head start in securing your long-term employment by investing in your future (if that is of interest to them). It is a calculated risk to divulge your long-term plans, but it is a move that can put you at an advantage.

* How do you know if your current organization is planning to invest in your future?
* How will you know when it is time for you to start job hunting (internally or externally)?
* What is your opinion on counter-offers? Is it flattering or an afterthought? Why?

REDEFINE THE IDEA OF LOYALTY. Suppress the need to protect the interest of the organization by hindering your growth potential. Loyalty should be earned, and it may or may not benefit you in the long run. It is in the best interest of a leader to make decisions that best serve their future; similarly, an organization must focus on achieving its vision and prescribed mission. In an ideal world, your goals will align with your organization's needs and therefore growth and opportunities will be created for a mutual benefit. Leaders become invested in their departments, teams, and superiors, and the ability to prioritize their own professional goals can become overshadowed by the desire to help and serve others. Career growth, obtaining desirable opportunities, and following your passion is a personal choice; you should always prioritize your interests.

Don't put unnecessary pressure on yourself by overthinking how to remain loyal. The good news is that if you are happy in your current organization and you see room for growth (activate the 'say it out loud' skill). Your needs are the priority.

* Have you ever stayed in a job longer than you wanted to out of loyalty? Why?
* Are you holding back (voice, talents, and skills) at work?
* What needs do you have that are not being met in your current role within your organization?

FINAL REFLECTION

* On a scale of 1 (poor) to 10 (superpower), how would you rate your confidence in advocating for your career interests?
* What challenges have you faced in past attempts to advocate for your professional growth?
* What opportunities may be present for you to consider after reading this chapter?

IN SUMMARY

ADVOCATE FOR YOURSELF AND NEVER SETTLE.
Choose to *say it out loud, be calculated, and redefine the idea of loyalty.* This will ensure you are in a position to benefit from all potential opportunities.

SECTION II
THE DIRTY RULES

Power dynamics are constant in leadership. Every leader has a boss and while it is not often advertised, titles and rank are not always synonymous. Leading in an organization that has a hierarchical leadership structure (most power at the top, least at the bottom)can appear easy and straightforward; however, there are intricacies that are important to note. For example, the hardest relationships to build and decipher can be those with other leaders. As a leader you are expected to be able to appease, partner, and support a myriad of individuals who are in various positions of power within your organization. It can be daunting to cater to the needs and requests of your direct supervisor and other leaders. Leaders need to be agile and always ready to serve multiple masters.

Workplace trauma is another taboo subject in leadership that is downplayed and often made to seem incidental while it is habitual and frequent in occurrence. Many leaders have personally experienced trauma inflicted by colleagues, subordinates, superiors and others that they interact with on the job. They may face unexpected, shocking, and uncomfortable situations over their career trajectory. Leaders who choose to reflect and cope by focusing on self-care and recovery in order to heal will face an advantage over those who suppress their emotions. You should expect to face difficult circumstances. In your position, you will be expected to make timely decisions during unnerving situations and your integrity will be judged by those who report to you and/or your peers and therefore your ability to respond professionally is of utmost importance.

In order to maneuver through these difficult interactions, you should develop and use coping strategies to deal with workplace stress. Previously experienced workplace trauma can be akin to post-traumatic stress in that newly occurring trauma can unleash feelings of past traumatic events. These experiences can feel terrible while they are happening. With skillful reflection and the opportunity to process the situation, in the aftermath you may have a revelation that can ultimately lead to a new perspective on past events and foster an increase in your ability to respond in a way that affirms your self-worth and builds influence in the future.

We all learn something different from transformative experiences. It is important that you grow from trauma and refuse to dwell and drown in fear and anger. Self-awareness and reflection can be helpful in processing events that are out of your control. A metamorphosis can occur as you transform from a complacent leader to a self-fulfilled leader, but it requires honesty, courage, and determination.

Workplace injustices include micro aggressions, systemic inequities, and mistrust. When faced with these obstacles, your objective is to regain control and move beyond your current circumstance.

Learn to Master the Dirty Rules

In the upcoming chapters, prepare to learn how to remain agile while protecting your dignity during times of uncertainty. The rules in this section address trauma that can occur due to power dynamics amongst leaders. The skills shared encourage the development and utilization of coping mechanisms to navigate unforeseen circumstances in the workplace.

Rule 4: STAND TALL WHEN OTHERS FALL SHORT

SKILLS	
	Lead with integrity.
	Control your reaction.
	Pass the test.

Rule 5: BAD THINGS CAN HAPPEN TO GOOD PEOPLE

SKILLS	
	Expect the unexpected.
	Master the lesson.
	Recover in motion.

Rule 6: THERE IS NO SUCH THING AS A WORKPLACE SAVIOR

SKILLS	
	Reject the status quo.
	Trust your gut.
	Channel your belief.

4

"This is not brain surgery!"
STAND TALL WHEN OTHERS FALL SHORT

Madison sat in her office staring at the wall. She was a month into her new position as the director of a busy orthopedic practice. It was her dream job that came with a comfortable salary to match. Five managers reported to her, and she was responsible for three office locations spread across an assigned geographical region. She had chosen to relocate to a new state for this job and was excited about exploring this new area with her husband, Nathan. He worked in a full-time remote position and so the transition had been smooth for them.

The interview process for the position had been extremely intense-more than six rounds of interviews that included meeting with 12 members of the local and extended leadership team. During the interviews, Madison shared her eagerness to bring her expertise onboard. It was unanimously agreed that she was the right person for the job. She quickly accepted the offer, and six weeks later she and Nathan drove across country to their new home in the Midwest.

Initially, the physicians who she met with were excited about her diverse background and experience. They were interested in her ideas and the innovations that she would bring to the organization.

But exactly six months later, Madison was frustrated and rethinking her decision to take this job.

From the start, she had been personable. She spent most of the first few weeks getting to know the staff and the physicians at each of her practice locations. Madison prided herself on building influence across teams and knew that success was contingent on establishing key relationships. Although everyone was polite during scheduled one-on-one meetings, she started to hear rumors that they thought she was pushy and too keen on changing things.

Madison was a little taken aback. Wasn't this the very reason that she had been the lead candidate during the job search? They were clearly impressed with her past positions in large, complex organizational settings in the Northeast, and appreciated that she was used to fast-paced environments and unexpected change.

Over the next few months, Madison spent much of her time learning the ropes of the department. While she'd identified many areas that would benefit from having policies established or reviewed, she purposely had not made any changes during her first 90 days. She had heard from her managers that staff grumblings were rampant. She felt a bit defeated. In past roles, she typically had buy-in from the physicians who she worked with by now.

Madison shared her concerns during her weekly meeting with her new boss, Barron, an executive with oversight of all ambulatory care sites for their health system. Barron listened earnestly and reassured Madison that gaining traction with this group would just take some time. They were used to the leadership style of her predecessor who had been at the helm for a decade and had retired a few months before Madison joined the team. After the meeting, Madison felt better and decided that she would follow Barron's lead. He seemed to understand the culture of the organization. So she had remained positive, certain that things would eventually change for the better as she earned the trust of the team.

A knock on the door broke Madison's train of thought. She wondered how long she had been daydreaming while staring at her office's dated wallpaper.

She chose not to respond to the knock because she needed a few more minutes to regain her composure.

Madison glanced at the time on the computer, realizing that she typically would have rounded on the staff by now, but she could not muster the energy to get up from her seat. She was still shocked at the scene that played out earlier that morning in the team meeting.

Madison had arrived at 7:30 am with coffee and donuts for the monthly all staff meeting. She knew that sugar was always welcome during these mandatory meetings. The office did not open for another hour, and the meeting was being held in the vacant waiting area of their largest office practice. Sixty staff members gathered, loudly gossiping and enjoying their free breakfast, as they waited for Madison to call the meeting to order. Madison really enjoyed the new team. Under Madison's guidance, the meetings had evolved from eclectic complaint sessions to interactive discussions that often included learning in-services from various personnel based on the team's request.

She had a full agenda and urgently called the group to order. All levels of staff—except the physicians who had a competing meeting at the same time—typically attended. The monthly meeting was the perfect opportunity for staff to feel comfortable enough to ask key questions and to ensure that they were clear about policies, procedures, and the needs of the practice.

Time always flew during these meetings. Before Madison knew it, they were down to the final 15 minutes when she typically hosted a Q&A session called 'Ask Me Anything' to encourage the staff to engage and ask questions without judgment.

"Okay, it's time for your favorite portion of the meeting," she teased. She stood up and walked to the front of the room. "Time to grill the boss, whatcha got?" she said as she relaxed her stance, leaning lightly against the podium.

Belinda, one of the newer medical assistants raised her hand. Before Madison could acknowledge her question, one of the physicians strolled to the front of the room. Madison rolled her eyes and softly swore under her breath.

Dr. Laura Joy was nothing like what her name implied. She was always angry and complained about everything.

"I have a question Madison," she said.

The sound of her voice made Madison cringe.

Without giving Madison a chance to acknowledge her presence, Dr. Joy continued.

"Why is it that you can't do your job? Why is it that even though you know that my calendar is supposed to be blocked every Wednesday, it is not?" Her voice grew louder, and she walked toward Madison. She strolled toward the front of the room, not stopping until she was barely a finger away from Madison's face.

"Dr. Joy, I am happy to investigate this matter, once my meeting concludes," Madison said. She tried to keep her voice pleasant and regain control of her meeting.

Dr. Joy was not satisfied. "No! No, you will not take care of this later. You will take care of this now!" her voice rose as she glared at Madison. "I don't understand what is so hard about blocking my schedule, Madison!" she snarled.

The assembled staff looked on in shock. Madison stood stock-still for a moment. She could not believe what was happening. Scheduling errors were not a crisis. She measured her words.

"Dr. Joy, I am happy to disc-"

"This is not brain surgery!" Dr. Joy cut her off, stepping even closer. "You need to do your job or get out!" Spit formed in the corner of her mouth as she screamed.

Madison took a step back and turned to one of her managers, giving her a telepathic look that said, *take over while I remove this crazy lady from our meeting,* and tried to walk away.

Unsatisfied, Dr. Joy followed on Madison's heels. Madison left the room and turned a corner, waiting until she was out of earshot of the meeting to speak.

"What is your problem?" she asked. Her eye twitched. "That was completely inappropriate."

Dr. Joy doubled down. "My schedule is not blocked," she hissed, spun on her heels, and walked off. Madison stood in the hallway, hoping that her facial expression did not reflect the outrage flowing through her body.

She walked into her private office, closed the door, and immediately turned to her computer to investigate the issue. Within seconds, she found an email from Dr. Joy requesting that the schedule be unblocked and open on the date in question.

A slew of curses escaped Madison's lips. Not only had she been disrespected in her meeting, but Dr. Joy had been wrong all along. Madison wanted to print the email and shove it in her face in front of the staff, but deep down she knew she couldn't do that. So here she was an hour later, staring at dated wallpaper still waiting for her blood pressure to decrease, and ignoring the knocking that persisted at the door.

Had she made a mistake relocating to a new state for this job? It didn't matter. The choice was made. She would have to stick this out for better or worse (at least for now). Her thoughts swirled in her head as she thought about what to do next. Thirty minutes later, she printed the email and made her way to Dr. Joy's office.

Madison found her in an exam room with a patient. She hung out in the hallway hoping to catch the doctor before she moved to her next patient. Finally, Dr. Joy emerged from one of the exam rooms with a seemingly friendly manner.

"Madison?" she said. Her voice was polite, but she did not stop walking.

How could the woman be so calm and casual as if she had not just disrespected Madison in front of the entire team? Madison said a silent prayer to refrain from doing something she would regret as she followed Dr. Joy into her office.

"I wanted to show you this email." Madison handed over the printed message as she spoke.

The doctor's eyes scanned the email, her face unmoving. She cleared her throat. "I actually saw this after we spoke this morning," she said casually.

"Spoke?!" Madison sputtered.

"After our conversation, I searched my email and found this message that reminded me that I did ask to see those patients." She paused, glancing up at Madison. "Thanks for bringing this to my attention." Dr. Joy turned back to her computer screen.

Madison felt the steam rising from her body. She knew better than to waste her time trying to get the physician to offer an apology. She had learned long ago that she could not control other people; she could only control herself. Madison had a million curse words and snarky comments that would have been perfect in this moment but instead, she said nothing. She chose to walk away and be the bigger person.

POST-CHAPTER REFLECTION

* What stood out for you in this story?
* How would you feel if you were belittled and embarrassed in front of your staff and other team members?
* What is Worse: Working with a person in a position of power who does not show you respect in the workplace *or* choosing to respond professionally although the other person chooses to be raw and relentless.

THE BOTTOM LINE

Incivility is common in the workplace and has been for centuries. In the ideal world, attaining positional equity would be a priority in organizations; however, this is rare. Positional equity can be achieved by establishing a workplace culture that respects all staff equally and consistently applies equitable behavior standards across the organization, regardless of power dynamics. Titles, positions, and roles within an organization matter and some individuals choose to abuse their power in the form of bullying with offensive and unsociable behavior. As a leader, it can be shocking and appalling to be on the receiving end of inappropriate communication and behavior from peers, superiors or those that fall in-between in matrix organizations. Incivility is not acceptable in any professional environment.

WHAT YOU NEED TO KNOW

> Leadership can have its ugly moments. Powerful lessons can be learned in the aftermath of conflict. You can gain clarity and a refined understanding of how to both protect your dignity and make the right choice during jarring interactions at work.

The following skills can help you align your best interests and intentional approach to handling difficult situations:

SKILLS	
	Lead with integrity.
	Control your reaction.
	Pass the test.

The reflective prompts shared throughout this chapter are designed to help you consider your purpose and expectations that you are hoping to achieve as you intentionally utilize these techniques.

LEAD WITH INTEGRITY. It takes courage and commitment to your core beliefs and values. You have a duty to remain professional and to respond appropriately despite the intensity of the situations that you may face. The workplace heightens the need for you to embody the principle endorsed by former U.S. First Lady, Michele Obama: "When they go low, you go high." Leadership integrity is making the right choice in the height of a crucial situation in the workplace. The right choice may leave you feeling inadequate, defeated, and embarrassed. The harsh truth is that leadership integrity is not intended to protect or inflate your pride. The good news is that maintaining leadership integrity can help you to relentlessly display high levels of emotional intelligence. This will stretch you mentally and can startle those who have positional or functional power in the workplace. Remain strong and know that despite the challenges or situations you may face in the workplace, you have the strength to overcome.

* What type of leadership legacy do you want to leave in your organization?

* How can you demand respect in the workplace while simultaneously demonstrating strong leadership qualities?

* What helps you to do the right thing during tumultuous situations in the workplace?

CONTROL YOUR REACTION. You can always control your actions and response despite any challenge you may face in the workplace. Reactive behavior can be a knee jerk response during conflict. Reactions can be verbal, non-verbal, direct, in-direct, passive, aggressive or a mix of these. As a leader, the way you respond to conflict matters. It is important to disconnect your emotions during intense situations so that you can think critically and professionally. Although it is natural to want to mimic the energy, words, or actions directed at you, as a leader your job is to maintain calm, cool, and collected in times of duress. Practice demonstrating restrained emotion, highly collaborative techniques in low-stakes environments so that you are prepared to execute flawlessly during critical situations. Achieving this takes planning, practice, and purpose.

* What would it look like for you to be the 'bigger person' during conflict?

* How can you find the balance between what you want to say and the point that you need to get across?

* How would a mentor/leader that you look up to handle this situation?

PASS THE TEST. Leaders face people, situations, challenges, and circumstances that can be incomprehensible. Maintaining equilibrium takes agility, confidence, and humility. Regardless of your title in an organization, you will be tested. You may feel disrespected, belittled, excluded, attacked, abused, and (insert feeling). If you silently wonder *if* you are being tested, then the answer is yes! Much like a pop quiz, you need to be prepared at all times to pass the test. Your leadership integrity is being questioned in these unexpected situations and your grade is reliant on your ability to reject poor behavior and choose to perform by rising above the drama. Do what you need to do to make the right choice in trying times. Welcome the chance to practice and perfect your response to the challenge. Lean in and get uncomfortable.

* How do you determine when to ignore or when to address an uncomfortable situation at work?

* What approach have you used during a difficult conversation that has led to a successful outcome?

* What coping mechanisms do you use to manage stress that may arise due to workplace conflict?

FINAL REFLECTION

* On a scale of 1(poor) to 10 (superpower), how would you rate your ability to stand tall when others fall short in times of workplace conflict?
* What challenges have you faced in responding to workplace conflict?
* What opportunities may be present for you to consider after reading this chapter?

IN SUMMARY

STAND TALL WHEN OTHERS FALL SHORT. Choose to *lead with integrity, control your reactions,* and *pass the test.* This will ensure that your intentions and actions align in the workplace.

5

"My hands are tied."
BAD THINGS CAN HAPPEN TO GOOD PEOPLE

Madison pulled into the parking lot at work in the best mood that she had been in for months. This was her first day back to work after spending seven days in a gorgeous Caribbean country to celebrate her fifth wedding anniversary. She'd done nothing but relax on the beach with her husband and people watch, one of their favorite pastimes. She was not only relaxed, but also excited. Things were good. Madison was happy and had everything she wanted—at home and at work. She could not have predicted that she would feel so content in both environments.

So much had transpired in her career over the past five years. Madison had a fantastic working relationship with her boss, Barron. He had coached and developed her as a novice director. A year into her position, he decided to leave the company for a Senior Vice President position on the East Coast. Ironically Barron was moving to the same organization where Madison had started her career. Barron asked her to rejoin the organization as his Director of Operations. Madison accepted and she and husband, Nathan, happily moved back home to the Northeast, closer to family. It was a full circle moment to be back in the place where she'd first learned the mechanics of management as a supervisor and now, she was running an entire division and was one position removed from the same CFO that she used to fear back in the day.

Madison got out of her car and casually tossed her keys to the parking attendant.

"Have a good day, Mrs. Hopeton." He caught the keys with one hand.

Normally, Madison felt sluggish in the mornings, but today she was energized. She power-walked the ten city blocks to reach the office. She felt free and content and forced herself to slow her pace and take in the scenery. The tree-lined streets were jam-packed with cars and yellow taxis. People walked briskly, heads down, intent on getting to their destinations. Central Park lay ahead in the distance.

Usually, Madison wouldn't have given the trees a second glance, but today, she admired their beauty.

A fresh outdoor smell hung in the air. She took in the sights as she walked up Fifth Avenue and dreamed of being rich enough to renew her wedding vows in a lavish ceremony in the park, fantasizing about creating memories in a place that was beloved by many.

She approached her favorite coffee cart and dug into her cross-body purse to retrieve her wallet. She greeted Ross, the cart owner, with the wide, warm, welcoming smile reserved for those in her inner circle.

"Mrs. Hopeton, you're back!" Although she worked in a city with over 8 million people, her coffee guy always remembered the names of his favorite customers. Madison loved this and thought it was the epitome of good service.

"I am," she replied, a hint of sadness in her voice.

"I checked the numbers on the lotto website, and I didn't hit big yet, and so I am stuck working for now," she joked.

"Maybe you'll hit it big next time," Ross grinned, turning to prepare her medium coffee. Madison didn't even have to tell him. Ross remembered her as the 'light and sweet' person. He always joked about how the "real" coffee drinkers would consider her order a dessert.

Ross placed her coffee in a holder, and then paused, selecting a breakfast to go with her beverage—it was a routine they'd shared for years.

He made his choice and handed Madison a brown bag folded at the top, leaving breakfast as a surprise for her to discover once she got to the office.

He smiled appreciatively as he picked up the five-dollar bill that Madison had already placed on the counter.

Madison sipped her coffee as she approached the office building. She swiped her badge for access to the main entry way, then jogged to meet the waiting elevator. It was already full but Madison squeezed in. The passengers shifted reluctantly to make space. Buttons to every floor were pressed. Madison silently sipped her coffee and waited for the elevator to slowly make its way to the 10th floor.

Barron was the first person she spotted when she walked through the office doors. She raised her hand to wave, but he barely acknowledged her. He gave her a nod, turning his attention to his phone. Madison shrugged it off and headed into her office, ready to turn her attention to the hundreds of emails that would be in her inbox and thankful for the glazed donut that Ross had chosen for her breakfast.

Forty minutes later, Barron knocked on her door. She looked up just as he stuck his head inside.

"Hey Madison, I know you are catching up, but I wanted to give you a heads up that I put some time on the calendar for us to talk this afternoon," he said.

Madison was surprised by the lack of enthusiasm in

his voice. That was not the Barron that she was used to. She did not have time to give it much thought. The day flew by and before she could blink, it was time to meet with Barron.

He was finishing a call when Madison arrived at his office. He waved her in, and she took the seat he pointed to, opposite his desk.

She glanced out the window as he finished his call and took in the beauty of day. Barron's office had a grand view of Central Park, and she could get lost in the colors, movement, and ambiance of the park.

Barron hung up the phone and then walked over to the office door and closed it.

"We need to talk," he said, returning to his desk chair. He spoke in a low, strained voice that he reserved for serious situations.

Madison intuitively knew this was not going to be good and shifted her demeanor into business mode.

"What's up?" Madison leaned in and took out her notebook.

"My hands are tied," he said. He locked eyes with Madison. "I just got word from Dan Kennedy that we have to eliminate your position." His words hit Madison like a slap in the face. Her vision blurred. Her palms began to sweat, and she dropped her pen.

"Why? I don't understand," she said, bending down to retrieve the pen from the floor. "We just closed on a large acquisition, and I literally just submitted a justification to finance to get approval to hire additional staff."

Barron's face was pale. Madison thought he might be sick at any moment and for a second, she was more concerned about his health than her job.

"Barron, what is going on?" she asked forcefully. He sat on the edge of his seat, adjusted his posture as if it would help him say what he needed to say.

"I respect you too much to lie to you," he said leaning in and lowering his voice.

"Apparently, Dan owes a favor to a member of the Board of Trustees who has a son that just graduated from Brown University. Dan was approached about having the young man join our leadership team. You know that Dan is not one to provide explanations. All I know is that he seemed really annoyed to be put in this position, and he told me that the decision had already been made."

Madison sat speechless. Her mind whirled. What she was hearing made no sense to her.

"Dan did say that he would support me in keeping you within the organization, which is great, but . . ." Barron's voice trailed off. He looked powerless and helpless.

Madison took a deep breath and tried to clear her thoughts. "How can a board member just decide to fire someone and employ their kid?" Madison asked.

This is crazy. Madison thought to herself. She had a lot of four-letter words she wanted to yell and scream but this was not the time or the place. "Barron, what are you going to do?" She looked him squarely in the eye.

He looked at Madison sympathetically, choosing not to insult her with comforting words. He took a deep breath and began to talk, but his words washed over her.

She refocused her attention, and heard Barron say for the third time, "My hands are tied."

Madison sat motionless.

"I am going to help you transfer into a position with our downtown office," Barron said. "I'm waiting on a call back from Peter White, the VP of the office on 34th Street. They have a position similar to yours that is open. I'll know more by the end of the day."

Madison stood abruptly. "Thanks, Barron, I appreciate the referral. Please keep me posted." She refrained from shouting all of the expletives which swirled in her head, instead she turned on her heels and walked out of the office. She just made it into the restroom stall before the tears started.

She was angry that she was so emotional at work. She did not want to be seen looking devastated in the office. Madison didn't know how long she spent in that corner stall, but once she composed herself, she walked over to the sink. She blotted her face with a paper towel, attempting to lessen the redness in her eyes and to cool her cheeks.

Back in her office, she didn't shut down her computer, check her calendar, or let Barron or anyone else know that she was leaving, she just left.

As she waited for the elevator, she tried to steady her nerves. She thought about her husband Nathan, and how happy they had been earlier that day. She'd had a suspicion for the past few weeks and had taken a pregnancy test that confirmed that she was pregnant with their first baby. She had planned to share the big news tonight at a family dinner, but now all she craved was a quiet night at home. She called Nathan, recommending that they hold off on sharing the big news. Nathan knew something was off by the sound of Madison's voice, but he didn't push for information.

The elevator reached the lobby, and Madison slowly walked to the parking garage feeling a strange sense of calm. She knew that she could not rely on Barron to protect her because his "hands were tied," but she knew Nathan would have her back. She also knew that she would overcome this roadblock just as she had done with every other obstacle that she faced in the past.

POST-CHAPTER REFLECTION

* What stood out for you in this story?
* How would you feel if you faced an unexpected position elimination despite being a high-performing leader?
* What is Worse: Having a leader who fails to advocate for you and protect you when it matters *or* the fact that high performance does not equate to job security?

THE BOTTOM LINE

A curveball is a term that can describe a situation or circumstance that you did not see coming—a surprising and unexpected event. Things can shift from good to terrible in the blink of an eye. Unexpected situations can leave you feeling confused, powerless, defeated, and traumatized. The aftermath of such trauma can feel worse if you are a leader who prides yourself on being strategic, analytical, and calculated. Often you may feel compelled to blame yourself. It is important to remember that you did not do anything wrong. It is difficult but important to find the lessons in these moments in order to grow from them. You can reclaim your power by taking away lessons from all experiences that you face in the workplace; especially those that are deemed shocking or distressing.

WHAT YOU NEED TO KNOW

> Leadership is unpredictable and full of twists and turns. Remember that although you cannot predict the future, you will recover and get back on your feet.

The following skills can help you feel prepared to manage uncomfortable situations:

SKILLS	
	Expect the unexpected.
	Master the lesson.
	Recover in motion.

The reflective prompts shared throughout this chapter are designed to help you consider your purpose and expectations that you are hoping to achieve as you intentionally utilize these techniques.

EXPECT THE UNEXPECTED. Navigating unforeseen situations can often be a lesson in agility. It is crucial that you continuously strive to be resilient. There is no such thing as ultimate control in the workplace. In your tenure as a leader, you will face unwelcome discussions and circumstances that may include involuntary termination, position demotion, unjust performance feedback or conflicting directions from a superior. Try not to spend too much time investigating the root cause of the issue, obtaining unhelpful feedback from others, or justifying your stance. Scale up your determination to move past unforeseen events with confidence by shifting your perspective and adjusting your expectations to accept improbability and illogical decisions. It may feel daunting now, but you will survive.

- ✳ How do you feel when things are beyond your control?
- ✳ How do you handle pressure-filled situations at work?
- ✳ Who can you vent to about work stress and drama?

MASTER THE LESSON. Choose to recalibrate your curiosity. Pity parties may be free, but they do little to empower you after a devastating blow to your ego. Depersonalize the situation by thinking broadly about the circumstance. You are not the first leader at your organization to feel betrayed, appalled, or confused, and you will not be the last. The challenge is to reclaim your power by not worrying about validating your innocence. Increase your future footing by taking the opportunity to learn from this moment.

- ✳ What helps you to recover after managing stressful situations at work?
- ✳ How do you move beyond your gut reaction to a traumatic event at work to arrive to a place of reflection and intention?
- ✳ What skills can you elevate to support you as you rebound after a devastating workplace event?

RECOVER IN MOTION. Attempt to find stability as you continue moving forward and choose to intentionally process disturbing workplace events. Active recovery can put leaders at an advantage. But you have to reflect, heal, and take action simultaneously. Dictate the speed so that you feel comfortable, but keep in mind, stagnancy is not an option. Unfair and unjust experiences come with the territory. Dwelling on the things beyond your control is futile. Think about the good times ahead when you will be back in good spirits. Remember why you chose to be a leader and lean on your passion and purpose as you overcome this moment of discomfort.

* What have you faced in your past that has made you stronger as a leader?
* What actions can you take to cope with stress while strategically moving forward after facing a challenging situation at work?
* What advice do have for someone who feels discouraged as a result of unanticipated workplace trauma?

FINAL REFLECTION

* On a scale of 1 (poor) to 10 (superpower) how would you rate your ability to recover from situations that are beyond your control?
* What challenges have you faced that resulted from an unexpected situation?
* What opportunities may be present for you to consider after reading this chapter?

IN SUMMARY

BAD THINGS CAN HAPPEN TO GOOD PEOPLE. You should *expect the unexpected*, *master the lesson*, and *recover in motion*. This will ensure that you remain agile, prepared, and ready to overcome all unwelcome encounters.

6

"I am releasing your shackles."
THERE IS NO SUCH THING AS A WORKPLACE SAVIOR

Madison sat on the plush loveseat in the large corner office. She bounced her leg as she looked around, taking in the décor. The walls were painted a deep navy with white trim. The furniture was a dark mahogany, and the office had a masculine feel. There was limited wall art, aside from three framed diplomas that showcased degrees from Ivy League schools.

Madison tried to calm her nerves. She had felt confident when she requested this meeting two weeks ago, but now she wasn't so sure that it was the right decision. The knot that had begun in her stomach had traveled to her chest and had now arrived at her throat. *How was she going to get through this meeting?* She checked her watch. *Why was she feeling so anxious?*

Barron had graciously helped her secure a lateral position in the organization. Although she was furious about the circumstances, she understood that Barron had been powerless to fight the powers that be. She had quickly transitioned into the new role of Director of Community Operations. She'd now been in the role for 18 months.

She heard the sound of voices and footsteps approaching. She took a sip from a bottle of water, and she cleared her throat. After what seemed like an eternity, the company CEO, Chip Payne, walked into the office. He was a tall, oversized Caucasian man in his mid-fifties with a low haircut that was peppered with grey and starting to bald. He was known for his impassiveness, and you could never tell if he was pleased or annoyed during company meetings.

"Madison, thanks for taking some time to meet with me," his deep baritone was polite and welcoming, although his smile looked forced. He took a seat directly opposite her.

"I looked at your resume earlier today and it's quite impressive. Walk me through it."

Madison nodded and tried to quiet her nerves. She thought she was coming to talk about the significant issues she was facing as a leader in her department, but instead the CEO was starting the conversation as if this were a job interview.

"Sure." Madison said, shifting into her interview mode. She gave a concise description of her academic background and professional accomplishments, summarizing her experience as a team leader in various settings and organizations. He followed up with specific questions, asking her to share examples of her achievements in former jobs, as well as challenges and her strengths and weakness. Although Madison was puzzled by this line of questioning, it was not her first rodeo and she responded with ease. It was like a game of tennis. He served, and she returned the ball.

Finally, Chip ended the tennis match and addressed the elephant in the room. "What is going on in your service line?"

Madison paused to gather her words. She had rehearsed the night before to ensure that she did not leave out any pressing information and that her remarks did not come across solely as complaints. She took a sip of water and said, "I've been leading the Community Operations Division for the past 18 months, and I have major concerns."

His look intensified. He leaned in, motioning for her to share more.

Madison spoke about the lack of professionalism from the senior leadership, provided examples of systemic racism that appeared to be an accepted part of the culture, and expressed concerns about her boss,

Ryan King, who was a newer executive leader in the organization. Although she and Ryan met regularly, he had done little to address these concerns or support the solutions she recommended. Her impression was that he was afraid to address the underlying issues about the culture in the division and quietly accepted them because this service line was the top revenue maker for the organization. In three minutes flat, Madison made her case in a clear, concise, and competent manner. She knew what needed to be done to shift the culture and to eliminate the toxic culture, however she needed an executive sponsor to support her decision-making and direction.

Chip's expression was unreadable. His response while Madison spoke were murmured 'mmm's' and 'ok's.'

He stood as Madison finished and walked toward his desk, pausing to look out of the window. His 15th floor office had views of the FDR parkway and the bumper-to-bumper traffic below.

After about 60 seconds, he turned to his chair and sat down. "You have a hell of a background, and you seem like you know what you are doing. What I hear you saying is that you have been unsupported in being able to sustain change in your department. You were once in chains, but I am releasing your shackles."

Madison blinked, not expecting such a matter-of-fact and slightly off-putting response. She tried to understand what his statement really meant and how it might impact things moving forward. *Was he attempting to be supportive despite his misguided choice of words?* Madison did not have much time to process because he stood up, indicating their time was over. Madison left the office feeling slightly confused, hopeful but, at the same time, uncertain.

Fast forward three months and Madison was escorted from her office by the head of Human Resources. The unscheduled meeting with Human Resources had included talk of a 'voluntary resignation' and a severance package that she was strongly encouraged to accept. Madison carried her work bag and a box of personal belongings to her car. Her previous meeting with Mr. Payne ran through her mind.

"I am releasing your shackles," he had said. Apparently having no shackles meant having no job. She sighed and got behind the wheel of her car. She would put it out of her mind for now. Thankfully, her mother-in-law was in town and was enjoying spending time with the family, especially her baby girl who was starting to walk and was highly active. Madison was not happy about how things had ended, but she felt composed and confident that she would overcome this tragic turn of events. Although she was disappointed, she remained optimistic as she mentally prepared for a night of job hunting.

POST-CHAPTER REFLECTION

* What stood out for you in this story?
* How would you feel if you spoke up about systemic workplace issues with a superior, and it came back to bite you?
* What is Worse: Taking a calculated risk that results in termination *or* enduring a toxic work environment with the inability to make necessary changes?

THE BOTTOM LINE

Speaking your truth and being vulnerable are calculated risks. It can be difficult to decipher the right route and it is a personal decision on how to determine when to let your voice be heard. It takes guts to go against the status quo. You have to make the right decision for yourself as a leader. There are no guarantees, limited protections, and no such thing as a workplace savior. Building strong relationships and garnering trust across senior leadership is encouraged but does not equate to job security. As you hone skills to elevate your leadership power, make decisions that speak to the core of who you are as a leader. Lead with conviction and know that you will land on your feet.

WHAT YOU NEED TO KNOW

Leadership is not for the faint of heart. Remember that adversity builds character. You owe it to yourself to do the right thing at the right time.

The following skills can help you demonstrate the ability to stand strong in the face of adversity:

SKILLS	
	Reject the status quo.
	Trust your gut.
	Channel your belief.

The reflective prompts shared throughout this chapter are designed to help you consider your purpose and expectations that you are hoping to achieve as you intentionally utilize these techniques.

REJECT THE STATUS QUO. Move beyond complacency. Stand firm in your beliefs and refuse to turn a blind eye to systemic challenges or toxic cultures in organizations. You will face discomfort as you reject and try to challenge the status quo. Many leaders choose the illusion of peace in lieu of the raw reality of the situation and the discomfort that it may bring. You know what is important to you and if you don't, continue to evaluate your purpose and passion as a leader. Be aware and ready to articulate your stance on poor behavior, toxic cultures, and misaligned organizational values that might not align with your leadership views. Make every effort to be brave, honest, and to drive change in a way that makes you feel safe and comfortable.

* What are some workplace challenges that you are aware of that need to be addressed?
* What holds you back from addressing systemic or toxic issues that occur at work?
* Which internal stakeholders can support you if you choose to speak up to address politically driven workplace issues?

TRUST YOUR GUT. Make an informed decision and figure out when to pull the trigger. Trust is complicated in the workplace. It takes a long time to build trust with individuals, and it's not a fail-proof relationship. It is essential that you trust yourself more than you trust other people. You know what your core values are, and you do not need to justify your actions to anyone else. Make every effort to make proactive decisions and request feedback frequently from internal and external sources. Allow others to provide insight but rest assured that the final decision lies within you. You decide when you need to take action. You will know when the time is right to have pertinent discussions and with whom. Trust that your voice has just as much power as that of someone who holds authority. Adjust your pace to your internal compass and move forward when you feel ready.

* How do you decide who you can trust with sensitive information at work?

* What fears or concerns hold you back from speaking with senior leaders about toxic workplace issues?

* What will help you know when and if you should raise concerns about systemic issues?

CHANNEL YOUR BELIEF. Standing firm in your convictions can help you get through uncertain times. We all have different ways of processing and handling the aftermath of an unexpected event. Some people choose to rely on faith, spirituality, intuition, experience, religion, or other measured ways of believing that they can and will get through situations. We instinctively make meaning of situations and circumstances based on what we choose to believe during times of uncertainty. Choose to reflect on what helps you remain stable, encouraged, and safe during times of crisis.

* How do you overcome tough times?

* What are your thoughts about uncertainty/ambiguity in the workplace and how does it impact your ability to lead?

* How do you shift your mindset to remain positive in the face of despair?

FINAL REFLECTION

* On a scale of 1 (poor) to 10 (superpower), how would you rate your comfort level challenging the status quo?
* What challenges have you faced by standing firm in your convictions?
* What opportunities may be present for you to consider after reading this chapter?

IN SUMMARY

THERE IS NO SUCH THING AS A WORKPLACE SAVIOR. Choose to *reject the status quo*, *trust your gut*, and *channel your belief*. This will ensure that you remain true to your core values as a leader.

Section III
THE RULES OF THUMB

The leadership journey can be smooth sailing for some and tumultuous for others. Although leaders will have traveled distinctive paths, there is a commonality, which is the need to recognize that your leadership journey is original and unique to you. Everyone will not share your experiences, nor will they learn the same lessons. You may not get to choose what comes your way, but you can choose to accept or reject people, places, and ideas presented to you if they do not serve your needs and core values.

As you craft non-negotiable terms on how you choose to interact with all levels of leadership, as a leader you will realize that you do not need permission to display your intelligence and abilities. You will become more comfortable with using your voice. You may have experienced some lows along the way but be confident in your ability to traverse the roads that are less traveled.

Imposter Syndrome and systemic exclusion due to bias can cause 'rock stars' like yourself to hoard dynamic ideas and recommendations. You may be ready for career growth, but might hesitate to put yourself forward for roles that stretch you as a leader. Remove doubt and do it anyway. You don't turn down opportunities, you turn down job offers. You are in the driver's seat, and you can assess and reject positions that do not meet your requirements. Keep your options open and master your insecurities by moving beyond fear into opportunities to grow toward your career ambitions. Share your expertise, fresh view, and perspectives. Do not underestimate your power and contribution.

Many leaders have difficulty with expressing authenticity and struggle to meet workplace pressures while staying true to themselves. Authentic leadership can be hard. It is standing up when everyone else is sitting down. It is speaking up when others choose to be quiet. It is walking away because you deserve better. It is choosing mental health over money. It is choosing to remain optimistic despite traumatic incidents. It is standing alone in your convictions when it really matters. It is choosing yourself above all else.

There is a direct correlation between leading in a way that makes you feel comfortable and gaining influence in the workplace. Leadership power can accelerate your ability to sustain successful outcomes. This type of power is earned over time and can be measured by the trust, respect, and confidence that others associate with your professional abilities and personal character.

Every leader begins to become aware and intentional about using talents to contribute to the organization. With practice and intention, you will feel more secure in who you are as a leader. When you know your worth as a leader, you begin to contribute your knowledge, skills and recommendations without hesitation. As you grow professionally, you become self-aware, and you become clear about your non-negotiable needs in the workplace. You become comfortable in demonstrating your power by demanding respect from all levels of leadership as a requirement of employment. Consider scheduling one-on-one meetings with your leader to discuss your development and to ensure you are both clear on your impact and work performance. Being comfortable in your leadership abilities can lead to routine recognition from senior leaders and admiration from peers and novice leaders.

LEARN TO MASTER THE RULES OF THUMB

In the upcoming chapters, prepare to learn how to demonstrate confidence in your abilities to activate your leadership power. You have chosen to 'trust the process' and at this leadership stage, it is important to promote your mastery. The rules in this section address the importance of self-worth as a leader. The skills shared will promote the need for all levels of leaders to feel empowered to manage up, sideways, and diagonally in the workplace.

Rule 7: PROMOTE YOUR BRAND

SKILLS	
	Hold your head high.
	Prioritize your growth.
	Celebrate in advance.

Rule 8: EMBODY YOUR SUPERPOWER

SKILLS	
	Title does not equal ability.
	One size does not fit all.
	Show off your talents.

Rule 9: ALLOW OTHERS TO FILL YOUR BUCKET

SKILLS	
	Store the memory.
	Embrace vulnerability.
	Pass it on.

"Effective Immediately"
PROMOTE YOUR BRAND

One week had passed since the infamous "effective immediately" email had gone out to Madison's team. Her cell phone had been blowing up with messages from her concerned employees, colleagues, and even her old boss, Barron. She had given herself 24 hours to feel sorry for herself and spent almost two hours on the phone venting to her dear friend Shaina, who had remained Madison's confidant throughout her leadership climb. Shaina now lived in California. She had left the management world and worked in pharmaceutical business development.

It was Wednesday morning, and the house was eerily quiet. Her mother-in-law had returned to her home in Connecticut. Nathan was in his home office and their daughter was at daycare. Madison's mind was everywhere but focused on job hunting. She thought back to the three managers that she had worked for early in her career. They were all women who had been walked out of the office in the same way that she was last week. Their images appeared in her mental rolodex one by one as if she was watching a movie.

↶

She recalled Kelly, the White woman in her mid-30s, who was the bubbly, ambitious, and eager type of boss. Then there was Lorraine, the Black woman in her late 30s, who was the friendly, effective, and efficient type of boss. And finally, Amber, the Hispanic woman in her early 40s,forties who was the sharp, quick-witted, and smart-as-a-whip type of boss. All three had been skilled, educated, and well-versed in their fields, yet for some reason they too had received a surprise visit from HR and were quietly escorted out of the office. Their staff, just like Madison's, had received an email with some iteration of "effectively immediately [insert name] is no longer working with XYZ organization. We thank her for her contributions and wish her well on her future endeavors."

Madison remembered the confusion she felt about why her leader was leaving. The first time it happened, she was a naïve employee, less than one year into her job working as a secretary. She enjoyed working with

Kelly and was totally caught off guard when she read the "effective immediately" email. She could recall the day like yesterday; it was midweek and certainly midday. It was busy and she was preoccupied with many tasks. She didn't notice when Kelly quickly walked past her with her coat on and her handbag on her shoulder. She did notice the email that promptly arrived in her inbox with the cryptic subject line that made her stop what she was working on. She read the email message ten times, waiting for the curt announcement to make sense. She looked at her colleagues on her right and left. They continued to work as if nothing had happened. Tears welled up in her eyes. She was not the sentimental type, and could not place the emotions she was feeling. She closed the email, grabbed her cell phone, went out to the hallway, and called Nathan (then her boyfriend). In hushed whispers, she discussed Kelly's departure.

When she returned to work the next day, she was surprised to see that Howard, a leader that intermittently visited their location was on-site and sitting in Kelly's office. Madison was never clear about his role, but she knew that he was a member of senior leadership. On his previous visits to the office, Madison always kept her distance but maintained her impeccable work ethic. By now, everyone had read the email and the rumor mill was running rampant. Surprisingly, there had been no meeting, no other emails, and Howard never mentioned Kelly. It was as if she had never been a manager in the office. This infuriated Madison. She felt sad that Kelly had clearly been terminated from her position despite the email's vague language. She empathized with Kelly's likely feelings of humiliation and irritation that she was not given a chance to say goodbye to her team or the opportunity to defend her honor on the way out of the door.

Madison's normally upbeat disposition had shifted into anger and resentment based on a situation that did not involve her. She completed her tasks as normal, but it was obvious to others that something was wrong. After lunch, on her way back to her desk she saw Howard standing in the hallway. She gave him a polite hello and tried to walk past.

"Hey Madison, do you have a minute?" he asked. Madison slowed her pace, replying "of course." Her chest tightened and she got an instant headache. She felt nervous and slightly scared that today might be her turn to be walked out the door.

"Let's go to my office," he said, walking into the office that had been *Kelly's*. Madison followed. Once in the office, Howard closed the door and took a seat at the small table. She followed his lead and sat opposite him. She realized that she had never had a private meeting with Howard. The intimacy of the meeting space was nerve wrecking.

"We had to let Kelly go," Howard said, looking directly at Madison.

She nodded her head but did not reply. She was shocked that he was being so candid. She wasn't on the management team. *Why was he discussing this with her?*

"I know her departure was unexpected. I want you to know that you are doing a wonderful job and that Kelly's leaving will not affect your growth with us. I've been watching you, and I value your work."

Madison smiled, eyes wide, and nodded in appreciation. It took a second to find her voice. "Thank you." *What was going on?*

Howard turned to pick up his coffee from his desk. As he took a sip, the quiet in the room brought Madison back to attention. Howard did not seem to notice her bewilderment and continued on, "I wanted to speak with you for two reasons. The first is I want you to know that the decision on Kelly's employment predates your time here. While it is sad to see a colleague go, I hope you can understand that we can't share details." He paused to give her time to respond.

Again, she was at a loss for words. He smiled at her in a genuine fatherly way. She relaxed, and some of the tension she'd been holding left her shoulders. He leaned in closer. "I heard you were finishing your graduate studies. How much longer do you have?"

Talking about her achievements always excited Madison. "I'm finishing up my last class as we speak!"

"That's great news," he said.

Madison was pleased that he sounded so interested in her academics but was slightly curious as to why he cared.

"That's perfect. That leads me to the second reason I wanted to speak with you. I've heard wonderful things about your performance, dedication, and interest in management. As soon as you complete your degree, I'd like to promote you into a supervisor position." He paused and looked at her with a satisfied grin.

"Really!" Madison almost squealed.

"Yes. My plan is to announce that you will serve as the interim Supervisor until you complete your coursework, and then I would like for you to formally replace Kelly."

Madison's head swirled. She was excited, she was anxious, she was worried, she felt disloyal, and she was scared.

"That sounds great," she whispered.

"I know that a lot is happening quickly. I hope you're interested and will accept the offer." He leaned back in his chair with a sly grin satisfied with executing his mission of 'Fire Kelly and Promote Madison.'

"Yes, of course, I accept." Madison could hardly believe it.

Howard looked pleased. "Great. So it's settled." He

stood up from his chair.

They exchanged pleasantries and then as Madison headed out of the office, and it hit her. It wasn't his office or Kelly's office; this was going to be *her* office- "effective immediately."

∽

Madison's email chirped bringing her back to current day. She took a deep breath and opened her laptop. Her eyes widened and she leaned in to read the new message that had arrived. A recruiter from an organization that she had always wanted to work for had messaged her to coordinate an interview to discuss a leadership role. She closed her eyes, grateful for the job lead. Madison knew that despite this setback, she would secure a job that she deserved.

∽

POST-CHAPTER REFLECTION

* What stood out for you in this story?
* How do you feel when you are not privy to information on why a high-performing leader is (voluntarily or involuntarily) terminated?
* What is Worse: Having a leader that you respect unexpectedly resign *or* experiencing career advancement while someone you know faces career turmoil?

THE BOTTOM LINE

Resilience is best learned firsthand. Watching the mistakes of others can serve as cautionary tales, but it doesn't hit home like your own experience. Going through painful situations can cause you to reevaluate life. After you've overcome challenges, you tend to look at the world differently and take less for granted. You learn that although you are not in control of circumstances, you will persevere. As a leader, you can use your knowledge, skills, and abilities to propel yourself forward in your career. Rebounding after a career setback can be taxing and elicit feelings of insecurity. Even though you may feel ill-prepared and exhausted, know that you are a valuable player–even off the court. Say "yes" to opportunity and "no" to doubt and fear.

WHAT YOU NEED TO KNOW

> Leaders must stay ready and strive to work to the top of their expertise (not title)! Remember that your character, actions, and work legacy are constantly being evaluated.

The following skills can help you learn to showcase your talents and remain optimistic despite your circumstances:

SKILLS
Hold your head high.
Prioritize your growth.
Celebrate in advance.

The reflective prompts shared throughout this chapter are designed to help you consider your purpose and expectations that you are hoping to achieve as you intentionally utilize these techniques.

HOLD YOUR HEAD HIGH. Even at your lowest, you do not have to be ashamed. Your circumstances have not tainted your talents and effectiveness as a leader. As you calculate your next move, feel assured that you will get another chance to shine. Reframe your situation by reminding yourself of your past accomplishments. You should not be embarrassed or worry about what other people think. Hold your head high and take advantage of every opportunity to showcase your leadership brand.

* Why is it important to always promote your personal brand?

* How can you persuade yourself to move forward when you feel defeated?

* What strategies can you use to remain motivated during times of turmoil in your career?

PRIORITIZE YOUR GROWTH. As a leader, your work ethic should exceed your current position. Strive to match the energy and skillset required for your ideal position. Continue to carry yourself with the utmost respect and focus on building quality relationships. You never know who might be gauging your professional resilience and, most importantly, who might advocate on your behalf when it matters.

Be aware that there is no such thing as a casual conversation with a senior leader. Your performance and abilities are always being evaluated and measured. Relationships—both inside and outside of the workplace can be essential to your career growth. Although for some, networking can feel intimidating, consider how to gradually become proficient without compromising your comfort zone. If you stay prepared by prioritizing your growth, you will remain ahead of the curve.

* How can collaboration and networking benefit your growth as a leader?
* How do you measure and evaluate your leadership impact in the workplace?

* What opportunities exist for you to step out of your comfort zone in an effort to prioritize career growth?

CELEBRATE IN ADVANCE. Remain motivated even if you do not see expected results within your desired timeframe. Constant evaluation and re-evaluation, planning for and managing change, and remaining agile come with the territory of leadership. You may have specific goals that you want to achieve, which can help to direct your steps. If you choose or need to pivot in your profession, having an idea of where you want to go or what you want to accomplish can help. A positive mindset can support you during times of uncertainty. Encouragement can come in the form of affirmations, coaching discussions, or advice from a trusted advisor to provide a few examples. Proactively celebrate your future opportunities as a means of envisioning your potential victory and take the steps to move your ideas into existence.

* What drives you forward when you feel stuck as a leader?
* How do acknowledge and/or celebrate your professional/career/workplace accomplishments?
* What steps can you take right now that will help you achieve your future career goals?

FINAL REFLECTION

* On a scale of 1 (poor) to 10 (superpower), how would you rate your aptitude to self-promote at work?
* What challenges have you faced when trying to build relationships and/or collaborate with your peers?
* What opportunities may be present for you to consider after reading this chapter?

IN SUMMARY

PROMOTE YOUR BRAND. Always *hold your head high*, *prioritize your growth*, and *celebrate in advance*. This will ensure that others notice that you are a high-performing leader and a valuable member of the team.

"You are already a powerful weapon and you're not even fully assembled."

EMBODY YOUR SUPERPOWER

"I am enough, and my power and influence will always shine bright. I am enough, and my power and influence will always shine bright." Madison repeated the mantra to calm her nerves. Sitting in her car, she was minutes away from one of the most important interviews of her life. After receiving walking papers from her last position, she had quickly landed a director position at a nearby competing organization. She had easily acclimated to her role with the company. Now, two years and another baby girl later, she was being considered for a Senior Director position. Madison knew she had the skills, credentials, and experience for the job. She also knew she was an underdog for the position because this Senior Director role had oversight of a branch specializing an area in which she had limited practice. Still, she felt confident in her abilities and excited for the opportunity to interview for this new role.

Madison glanced in the rearview mirror and tucked away stray curls. She wanted to ensure that her hair was in a perfect bun, arranged like a regal crown. She had five minutes to spare before the interview and used that time to pore over her preparation notes. She'd spent the weekend deconstructing her resume to ensure it addressed every aspect of the position description so that she could speak to her expertise and past roles to showcase how she would deliver high-value contributions for the company.

She took a deep breath and exhaled, shoving her notebook into an oversized tote bag and whispering a final reminder to herself: "You need me. I don't need you." A strange cockiness ran through her veins. She felt prepared and confident, she strolled toward the office building.

Madison arrived in the executive suite exactly three minutes early and greeted the executive assistant. She motioned Madison into the executive office. "Mr. Charles will see you now," she said. Madison followed. The older woman smiled warmly, reminding Madison of a proud auntie, and handed her a bottle of water and ushered her into an office.

Lance Charles, the Chief Operations Officer, was sitting casually at a table that took up most of the space in his modest office. He welcomed Madison in a non-committal manner, and gestured for her to sit down. "Good morning, Lance," Madison said. She felt calm and ready.

He started the conversation with routine pleasantries about the weekend, which provided a few moments for Madison to allow her mind to fully relax.

Lance shifted into gear, bringing Madison to attention. "Walk me through your resume," he said, sitting forward in a less relaxed, more formal posture.

Madison took a breath and decided to take a calculated risk by just being herself. Instead of proudly reciting the accomplishments, projects, and responsibilities that she had accomplished, she decided to share the story of her career highlights. As she spoke, she focused in on a few powerful stories that illustrated her ability to execute the assigned responsibilities. The experiences she shared demonstrated her ability to influence, lead, and maintain her integrity in the workplace despite challenging circumstances.

As she spoke, Madison watched as Lance's expression soften. His questions shifted from matter-of-fact to engaged curiosity as she told her story, and he noted her responses in his leather portfolio as she talked.

Madison radiated with self-confidence, knowing that she was crushing the interview. They talked for more than an hour. While Madison was ready for the interview to end, she knew that she would never have the opportunity to make a strong first impression with this senior leader again.

Lance transitioned the conversation to sustaining change within an organization. The company had recently merged with a competitor. Although they had spent a year trying to iron out the expected political drama in the aftermath, the company still struggled with consistency and standardization. Madison leaned in, taking in the information on current challenges in company.

As she listened, Madison became even more excited about the potential opportunity. As a leader, helping teams embrace change and adapt to innovative ideas was her sweet spot. When Lance paused for a breath, Madison took advantage of the moment to share her theory on how to best engage with individuals, teams, or organizations that struggle with change.

She made direct eye contact as she shared a metaphor comparing implementing change management principles to the removal of a bandage from a wound. The key to successful change management, she said, was to customize the approach to the individual. Just as removing a bandage from a wound could be traumatizing for some, for others it was relatively painless.

Madison stressed the importance of asking questions and over communicating small details to those that might be apprehensive or worried about the change process. She ended her story confidently, "That is how I have been successful in eliciting change in organizations. If you hire me, I will partner with you to ensure that this company meets our measures and outcomes, and continues to be seen as a world-class organization."

Madison stopped talking. Lance looked slightly puzzled. *Had she said something wrong?* He appeared to be studying her as if she were a rare specimen.

"Hmm," Lance crossed his arms and stood. "What a surprise. There is so much more to your background and expertise than I anticipated."

"Thank you," Madison smiled. "I'm glad I was able to share some things you didn't know about me."

"I'm certain there is room for you to grow here," Lance said as he watched Madison gather her things. "I am glad to have you on the team. You are already a powerful weapon, and you're not even fully assembled."

Madison smiled, thanked him for his time, and walked out of his office. As she strolled toward the elevator, she processed his last comment. Was it a compliment? He could see her value. She replayed the conversation as she waited for the elevator and as the doors opened, she realized that Lance had not complimented her! Instead he had issued a challenge. It was one she was ready to accept. She would welcome the chance to show him and the rest of the company just how powerful a weapon she could be.

POST-CHAPTER REFLECTION

* What stood out for you in this story?
* How do you feel when you think someone underestimates your talents and abilities as a leader?
* What is Worse: Not having the opportunity to validate your expertise *or* not accepting the challenge to display your strengths.

THE BOTTOM LINE

Your knowledge and ideas are unique. Your past experiences—both victories and failures—have shaped your abilities. You have collected the ingredients along the way, and you now have a secret sauce that can be considered your superpower. No two leaders are the same. As a leader, it is important that you choose to share your expertise and offer meaningful contributions in the workplace. Accept that you have worked hard to reach your professional position. When you approach conversations strategically, there is no such thing as being too smart, too vocal, or thinking too differently. Senior leaders want innovation, fresh ideas, and new approaches. Embrace your expertise, share your talents, and let your light shine!

WHAT YOU NEED TO KNOW

> Leaders intentionally use and display their strengths in the workplace. Leverage your passion, worldview, and perspectives in your leadership brand to help you achieve your desired outcomes.

The following skills can help you increase your comfort with using your voice:

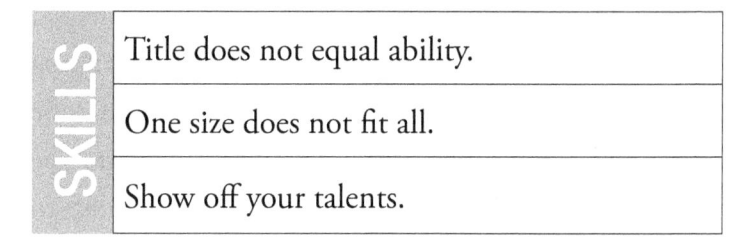

SKILLS	
	Title does not equal ability.
	One size does not fit all.
	Show off your talents.

The reflective prompts shared throughout this chapter are designed to help you consider your purpose and expectations that you are hoping to achieve as you intentionally utilize these techniques.

TITLE DOES NOT EQUAL ABILITY. Take advantage of opportunities that allow you to contribute recommendations and ideas in the workplace. Authority does not necessarily equate to knowledge. Depending on the culture of your workplace and the relationships you've developed, you may feel awkward asserting your opinions unless you are directly asked. Remember that you were hired for your skills and abilities. Be to share your superpower when you deem it appropriate. Remind yourself that your perspective has value and needs to be heard. Get out of your own way and don't hesitate to share information in your organization.

* What are you not saying/sharing that might be helpful at work?
* What is the worst thing that could happen if you step out of your comfort zone and assert your voice?
* What is your superpower as a leader?

ONE SIZE DOES NOT FIT ALL. Diverse ideas and approaches can be desirable and coveted in the workplace. Competition is fierce in every industry across the world, and there is no room for dated ideas. Diverse leaders bring creative, fresh ideas to the table. Your worldview is incomparable and can allow you to contribute to your organization in an extraordinary way. You have a seat at the table, an opportunity for empowerment. Challenge yourself to be bold and vocal. Leverage your past experiences and subject matter expertise.

* How do you muster the courage to elevate your voice and share both solicited and unsolicited ideas with your organization?
* What steps can you take to regularly contribute your perspective at work?
* What fresh or innovative ideas do you have that you have not shared?

SHOW OFF YOUR TALENTS. Regularly affirm your value and showcase your strengths. Your aim is to consistently demonstrate your value and skills by connecting your professional work to your subject matter expertise and experience. Bring forward skills and talents that may be unrelated to your current responsibilities, but presents a 360-degree view of your abilities.

Get comfortable with promoting your leadership brand in a positive way. Allow the people that work with you to know that you are a well-rounded person. You can choose to be your full self at work. You can elect to share your serious, quirky, suspicious, comedic, detailed, joyful, (insert here) side of your personality. Leaders are human beings, after all. Your distinctive traits can positively contribute to your ability to connect with your peers and others in the workplace. Embrace your uniqueness and enjoy the freedom of authenticity.

* What is it about your leadership approach that sets you apart from other leaders at work?
* What holds you back from achieving your desired goals at work?
* How would you modify your leadership style if you wanted to lead more authentically?

FINAL REFLECTION

* On a scale from (poor) to 10 (superpower), how would you rate your comfort at being fully authentic at work?
* What challenges have you faced when sharing diverse ideas or views at work?
* What opportunities may be present for you to consider after reading this chapter?

IN SUMMARY

EMBODY YOUR SUPERPOWER. Remember that *title does not equal ability, one size does not fit all, show off your talents*. This will ensure that your leadership abilities are showcased in a way that elevates your leadership power.

"Do you know how impactful you are?"
ALLOW OTHERS TO FILL YOUR BUCKET

The alarm clock sounded like a tractor trailer was reversing into Madison's bedroom. She hit the dismiss button to mute the noise and closed her eyes for another minute. It was 6:30 am and time to start her day.

Madison tiptoed into the bathroom, mustering the energy needed to brush her teeth and wash her face. She looked in the mirror, willing herself to recite an affirmation that would give her the strength to get through the day. Instead, she dressed as fast as a ninja, being careful not to disturb the rest of her sleeping family.

Twenty minutes later, she was settled at her desk in her home office with a steaming cup of coffee, preparing for the long day ahead. The past five years had been successful for Madison. True to her gut instinct, her interview with Lance Charles led to being hired into the Senior Director position. Recently, she was promoted to Vice President of Operations. The new position came with increased responsibility and challenges that Madison appreciated, as well as a handsome compensation package. Although her intense 12-hour workdays often felt like drinking directly from a fire hose, she felt professionally satisfied and grateful for the chance to continue to grow within the organization.

She reviewed her calendar as she finished the last of her liquid fuel and waited for its magic to kick in. It was 6:59am, so she joined her first meeting and didn't look up from the computer for the next two hours. She had a five-minute break before her next meeting, just enough time to see her children off at the bus.

Madison went in search of the family. As she approached the front door, she watched the chaos that ensued as her husband, Nathan, tried to get the kids out of the house and onto the bus.

She took a minute to observe him as he tried to remain calm as their daughters, ages seven and five, moved like sloths. The girls moved as if they had all the time in the world. They seemed to have a limited ability to hear and understand instructions. Nathan kept repeating "we are going to be late," but his words had no effect.

Madison stayed silent for as long as she could muster,

then finally decided to roll up her imaginary sleeves and made her presence known to the family. In a matter of three minutes, both kids had put on their shoes and backpacks and were walking out of the door. Madison kissed each girl on the head as they walked outside. She gave Nathan a coy smile and offered him a high five, to which he reluctantly returned and gave her a kiss on her head as he left the house to walk the girls to the bus. She felt proud of her mommy magic and quickly walked back to her office and logged into her next meeting, which was with her boss Lance.

Madison concluded the call one hour later and she realized that she had yet to have breakfast. She went to the kitchen, grabbed a yogurt, and ate it while she finished working on a project that was due later that afternoon. She had a two-hour break in her day and just as she was settling into some program planning, her phone rang. It was the school nurse at the children's school requesting that she pick up her youngest daughter who wasn't feeling well.

An hour later, she returned home from picking up her daughter and dropping her at her grandmother's house. After reading and resolving the issues in her email box, she checked the clock and saw that she had fifteen minutes to spare before her afternoon presentation to the board.

Before she could blink, the meeting was over. Madison sat in her chair feeling energized from a productive meeting with the board. The meeting had been intense and left her with a week worth of follow-up items.

Madison eyes were heavy, and she wanted to crawl under the desk to hide, but she had one more meeting. She sat enjoying the silence in the house and let her mind zone out. When she glanced back at the computer, the clock stated 5:31pm in bold judgmental red numbers. *Crap*, she hated when she was not on time and hurriedly joined the meeting.

Madison signed into the video call. She patiently waited a few minutes, until the Chief Information Office, Amy Bateman, hopped on the call looking like she had just run a marathon. Amy Bateman had joined the company six months prior. Madison was charged not only with bringing her up to speed on all the important accounts, but also was expected to train all of Amy's direct reports on the new technology that the company had purchased just before Amy's arrival. Over the past six months, Madison spent about 40 percent of her time working on projects that impacted Amy's area of responsibility—in addition to her own unrelated, competing priorities. The meeting was scheduled only a few days ago. Madison wondered if she had dropped the ball on something and for some strange reason felt nervous.

"Hi there," Amy said with a smile like she was greeting an old friend. "I really appreciate you taking this last-minute meeting."

"No problem," Madison said, immediately relaxed.

"Do you know how impactful you are?" Amy's calm expression was spotlighted on Madison's computer screen.

Madison gazed the screen, not exactly sure how to respond.

Amy continued without missing a beat. "I really want to say thank you for all that you have done for me and the team. Your work is phenomenal. You are always available. I've learned so much from you." A smile spread across her face. "I didn't mean to catch you off guard, but I wanted to share some real-time feedback about how grateful I am for you and all that you have done to date."

Madison smiled back at Amy, a little confused. She had never received such direct, unsolicited praise from a peer.

"Thanks, Amy. I am happy to help."

"Actually, you're doing more than was requested of you and, quite frankly, you've been more helpful than my boss."

"It's really no problem," Madison said, trying to move the conversation forward, away from herself. "Is there something else that I can provide for you?"

"No," Amy said, praising Madison for being such a valuable member of the team.

This encounter was a first for Madison. She had never experienced such thoughtful professional feedback outside of the performance evaluation process. She couldn't remember the last time she had been recognized and thanked for going above and beyond. Amy shared honest, detailed feedback, and Madison felt overwhelmed. Even though Madison boasted over a decade of experience as a skilled senior leader, this meeting had thrown her for a loop. Her eyes welled up. She did not know if it was because she was 11 hours into a full, exhausting day or if she was simply just touched by the gesture. Regaining her poise, she thanked Amy for her generous comments.

After the meeting ended, Madison settled into her chair, still absorbing Amy's call. It felt good to be seen. Madison took a moment to let the words of affirmation soak in. Moments like this validated her hard work. She had planned to start working on follow-up items from the board meeting and to check her emails before signing off for the night, but decided against it. There was no reason to ruin the moment. Instead, she took a moment to reflect on the fact that she was making great strides in her career now that she trusted herself to take charge and demonstrate her abilities. It felt good to know that she was thriving in all aspects of her life and so she chose to end the day in a place of gratitude.

POST-CHAPTER REFLECTION

* What stood out for you in this story?
* How does it make you feel when you receive unsolicited feedback from a person in a position of power?
* What is Worse: Feeling unseen *or* receiving positive feedback from everyone else except your immediate boss?

THE BOTTOM LINE

Leaders strive to be dedicated, knowledgeable, and selfless. You can easily fall prey to the thankless cycle of setting goals, working toward attaining the goals, achievement, and then repeating the sequence. Pushing forward, successfully executing, meeting or surpassing goals is the norm—recognition seems optional. Don't shy away when praise and grateful thanks come your way. As a humble leader, you may feel uncomfortable to receive words of appreciation and gratitude, but you deserve regular thanks for your arduous work and dedication. Welcome the love.

WHAT YOU NEED TO KNOW

Leaders deserve encouragement and praise. Remember that although management can feel like a thankless job, positive feedback affirms that you are hitting the mark.

The following skills can help you to intentionally allow others to fill your bucket:

SKILLS	
	Store the memory.
	Embrace vulnerability.
	Pass it on.

The reflective prompts shared throughout this chapter are designed to help you consider your purpose and expectations that you are hoping to achieve as you intentionally utilize these techniques.

STORE THE MEMORY. Keep the positive feedback that you receive in your mental filing cabinet because you will need to refer to it later. Requests, demands, expectations, and tasks typically outweigh words of encouragement, gratitude, and praise, which tend to be offered sparingly. Accept thoughtful comments and tributes as they come. As a leader, you know how hard you work, but it can be both humbling and educational to understand how you are being seen from an external viewpoint. Store the warm feelings of accomplishment that may surface. You will need to tap into that place when you feel disgruntled and overwhelmed. Leaders often travel over treacherous terrain and can fall into seemingly never-ending valleys; chances are you will be tired at points along your journey. Channel these positive memories of praise and appreciation when you are feeling defeated or discouraged. Hearing from others about your impact can help encourage and motivate you to keep moving ahead when you are exhausted mentally and physically. Allow others to spread the love. You deserve it.

* How can positive feedback boost your morale when you experience difficulties at work?

* How do you prefer to receive feedback (in person, in writing, in public, privately)? Have you shared this preference with others?

* Think about a time when someone shared a kind word about you that still makes you smile. What happened?

EMBRACE VULNERABILITY. Unsolicited feedback gives you the opportunity to understand how your actions, words, and leadership style are being received from another perspective. While some people welcome all types of feedback, for others unsolicited feedback may bring feelings of awkwardness and vulnerability. Privately reflect on the topics and situations that evoke emotional response or that may lead to feelings of vulnerability. You may want to assess your comfort level with being emotionally vulnerable in the workplace. Although healthy boundaries at work are of key importance, as a leader you may decide to allow others to see behind the curtain when appropriate. Authentic leaders experience moments of emotional vulnerability and do not associate sharing personal information with being weak or the inability to perform. It is okay to be your authentic professional self. Release the need to put on a mask and provide the space for others to fully appreciate the true essence of who you are as a leader.

* What level of vulnerability are you comfortable with in the workplace?
* How can you establish a healthy relationship with other leaders without sacrificing your personal boundaries?
* What should others know about you that will help them understand you better?

PASS IT ON. You should aim to reciprocate real-time praise to other deserving leaders in the workplace. Share honest, real-time feedback when it is deserved. Be sincere and let those that you believe to be impactful, hard workers know that you appreciate their dedication. Think about the leaders that you work with who are always ready to step up and help. A simple word of thanks can go further than you might imagine. Take the time to appreciate the people who make an impression on you. Real-time advice and positive comments feel genuine and can provide a satisfying boost to the person on the receiving end.

* What is the value of passing on positive feedback or praise to others?
* How often do you recognize others in real-time?
* How do you share feedback (in person, in writing, publicly, or privately)?

FINAL REFLECTION

* On a scale of 1 (poor) to 10 (superpower), how would you rate your comfort with accepting praise or positive feedback?
* What challenges have you faced with being vulnerable?
* What opportunities may be present for you to consider after reading this chapter?

IN SUMMARY

ALLOW OTHERS TO FILL YOUR BUCKET. *Store the memory, embrace vulnerability,* and choose to *pass it on.* This will ensure that you remain motivated to forge ahead on your leadership journey.

SECTION IV
THE ULTIMATE RULE

Leaders are master jugglers and can often multi-task with the best of them. Many want to lead by example and rarely acknowledge when they are overwhelmed. Depending on your position and level of responsibility, you may work long grueling days and feel unable to take time away from work. Keep in mind that there will always be a pressing issue or critical project deadline to be resolved. You may justify working 24/7 by thinking that you owe it to your team and peers who rely on you. After all, they need you to be available at any time, right? Wrong! It's time to shift your perspective and change your mindset.

Leaders often try to sustain a superhuman work ethic. But even the strongest leader needs to take a break from work. As a leader, you must advocate and demonstrate your own self-care. Leaders set the example. Be a leader who addresses self-care with the same rigor that you recommend to your friends, family, and peers.

Regardless of your stance on debates around work/life balance, leaders can acknowledge that they deserve rest, relaxation, and peace of mind. Allow yourself to set boundaries that support healthy habits.

As a leader, it is your responsibility to continuously assess and reassess the balance of the activities in your life. When you evaluate your purpose and passion, think about the fact that mental and physical health (e.g., stress, burnout, fatigue), and overall happiness are essential elements of the equation. Leaders who fail to align their priorities can be unstable and may be find themselves "running on fumes," unable to go the distance to accomplish their objectives. Find the balance, understand the importance of re-fueling yourself so you can protect, serve, and execute for your organization while honoring your needs simultaneously.

LEARN TO MASTER THE ULTIMATE RULE

In the final chapter, prepare to learn about the importance of setting boundaries as you calibrate your life balance. The rule in this section addresses the need to establish a sustainable work and life balance. The skills shared will promote the normalization of setting boundaries as a leader in the workplace.

Rule 10: EXHALE MORE THAN YOU INHALE

SKILLS	
	Find the balance.
	Self-care is a requirement.
	No is a sentence.

10

"*Remember to Breathe*"
Exhale More Than You Inhale

"Take a deep breath in to the count of three, and then exhale to the count of five." The comforting voice soothed the early risers who filled the small yoga studio at 6 am. Madison sat with her legs tucked under her, shoulders relaxed, and eyes closed. She followed the instruction's voice. Her mind felt clear and free as she focused on counting her breaths, trying to be in the moment. Every time her mind attempted to shift to her outstanding "to do" list, she would hear the yoga instructor say, "remember to breathe." On cue, Madison would force herself to inhale and exhale deeply, trying to eliminate all work, life, and non-yoga tasks from her mind. She exhaled deeply, the air escaping her mouth in a low, mechanical hum. This was her first full week of yoga in the morning before work.

She'd participated in a trial yoga class after listening to Shaina rave about how great she had been feeling since becoming a yogi in California. After Madison completed the free trial, she'd felt a sense of peace that she hadn't felt in years. She impulsively purchased a year-long membership plan, and tried to ignore the immediate sense of guilt over the cost and time commitment. But her recent inability to quell work-related panic attacks had persuaded her to bite the bullet and absorb the hefty price tag. She was constantly exhausted, and her family was noticing a shift in her personality. She was not showing up for them in the way that she wanted to, and she wanted to get back to herself. Madison decided to take a note from Senator Maxine Waters and planned to "reclaim her time" to reduce her stress level. High-priced or not, she needed the low-pressure and calming environment that this class offered.

Looking back, Madison remembered a time when she used to be comfortable asserting herself and had little difficulty prioritizing her wants and needs over those of other people. She was now 40 years old and happily married with two beautiful daughters. To the outside world, she led the perfect life. She was grateful for her blessings; however, she had been moving at such a fast, constant pace over the past decade that she knew burnout was a danger.

She still worked as the Vice President of Operations but now reported to the new COO, Rachel Cohen, who joined the team a few years ago. Rachel often relied on her to work long hours and on weekends to ensure the ball was not dropped on important projects. Initially Madison felt a sense of pride and responsibility to be selected as the point person for the senior leadership team. But when Rachel went out on leave for several months to finalize the adoption of her child, things really began to heat up in Madison's world. She kept her head down and said "yes" to any requests sent her away from the executive team. When Rachel returned to the office, Madison assumed things would revert to a place of normalcy. She quickly realized, however, that Rachel decided that because she was doing such a great job, Madison would continue as the primary contact for all executive and board-related needs. This now permanent responsibility would be in addition to her oversight of a busy service line. With no relief in sight, Madison decided to keep pushing forward. There didn't appear to be any alternative.

Outside of work, Madison served on the PTA and as a member of the Junior League. She helped, with various fundraisers raising money, planning, and/or attending events. She volunteered at the local shelter and spent the rest of her time shuttling her children to and from after-school activities and play dates. She was known as the Queen of "Get Stuff Done," both inside the office and at home. She could not remember the last time that she'd had a real vacation. She felt like it would be letting her team down if she took extended time off from the office. Although her family religiously set aside an annual two-week family-time vacation during the summer, Madison typically spent the whole time sleeping in her beach chair, exhausted from her daily activities.

The instructor's voice pulled Madison from her memories. "Remember to breathe." Madison silently swore. She'd allowed her mind to wander and swirl to a point where she felt confused, worried, and depleted all at the same time instead of being relaxed. She took several deep breaths and pondered why it was so hard to let go of all the air in her lungs.

After class, she took a long shower and decided to treat herself to breakfast at her favorite diner, which happened to be walking distance from the yoga studio. She worked a hybrid schedule and went into the office three times a week and worked from her home office two days a week. She typically arrived in the office by 7:30 am because that was the only way that she could enjoy her first cup of coffee in peace.

Not today, she said to herself as she sat down and ordered a coffee in addition to her classic comfort breakfast. She forced herself not to look at her watch or to check emails and to simply enjoy the moment. After breakfast, she headed to work.

She walked to her car two blocks away. As soon as she got in the car, her phone rang, and her friend Shaina was on the phone calling to invite her to the West Coast for her upcoming 40th birthday celebration. Madison had not seen Shaina in years. She wanted to support her, but she couldn't bear the thought of how much work it would take to plan for a weekend trip. She feigned soft interest and told Shaina that she would think about it. They abruptly ended the call when a work call came through. Unsurprisingly, it was one of her colleagues wanting to know if she could cover for him in a meeting planned for this afternoon. Madison quickly agreed and got off the phone. She drove twenty minutes to her office, parked in the garage and mentally prepared for the crazy day she was sure to have in the office.

As soon Madison walked into her office, Rachel popped in.

"Madison! I've been looking for you." Rachel's voice was just short of frantic.

Madison glanced at her watch to be sure that she hadn't misjudged the time. "Oh, hey Rachel. I decided to stop for breakfast."

"Can you attend the corporate banquet for me this Saturday? I can't go. I have some last-minute family things I have to do."

Rachel turned to walk away. "I'll send the details later."

Madison put her hand on Rachel's arm to stop her. "No," Madison's tone was sharper than she'd intended, but she was caught off-guard by the request.

Rachel turned around. "I am sorry, what?" Her face was filled with confusion. Rachel had worked with Madison for two years and had never heard her utter the words, 'I'll see,' never mind anything as definitive as 'no.'

"Is everything okay?"

Madison stood her ground. "Yes. I am okay. Tired, but okay. I'll be having a 'me day' on Saturday and so I can't attend the banquet for you. Sorry." Madison's voice was calmer now, but assertive.

"Oh, I understand," Rachel said, although she didn't mask her expression of confusion.

Madison held her breath. *She needed the self-care time she had planned, but had she gone too far?* "Thanks for understanding," she said. A thin smile crossed her face as she turned toward her desk. She felt proud of herself. Did Rachel get it? Madison hoped that Rachel recognized that she was setting a new boundary and would not challenge her.

The day flew by. When Madison looked up from her desk, it was already six o clock. Before leaving for the day, she decided to check her personal email. A Vegas-themed birthday e-invite from Shaina popped up on her screen. Madison sat looking at the invitation thinking about the fact that she was tired and wanted to have some fun. Before she could stop herself, she clicked open a new browser and purchased tickets to Vegas for her husband and herself to attend Shaina's party. Madison secretly felt giddy at her impromptu behavior. She never purchased tickets without detailed advance planning. She was also a stickler for getting a deal, typically spending weeks searching for the best airline price. But Madison knew she needed this. Nathan needed this. She was setting some new boundaries at work, and this vacation was a part of that. She logged back into her work email, blocked her calendar, and formally put in her PTO request for a full week.

She held her breath as she completed the seemingly clandestine deed. She inhaled and then instantly thought of the yoga teacher's prompt, "remember to breathe." This time, as she released her breath, she also let go of the need to be everything to everybody and inhaled the courage to choose herself.

POST-CHAPTER REFLECTION

* What stood out for you in this story?
* How do you feel when you are trying to be everything to everybody with no break in sight?
* What is Worse: Running at full speed 24/7 and feeling exhausted *or* not taking the time to set work and life boundaries?

THE BOTTOM LINE

Have you ever gone a day without noticing how you are breathing? What about a week, month, or year? You might fall into a pattern of moving through the days holding your breath and constantly inhaling and consuming. You might regularly inhale so deeply and frequently that you forget what it feels like to empty your lungs with a full, satisfying exhale. It is important to find the right balance between actively doing work and resting in an effort to recover from work. It is important to take time to notice your surroundings and become aware of how stress and tension is affecting your body. It is not healthy to operate in fight or flight mode 24/7.

You have to take care of yourself first. You deserve to incorporate regular non-work-related activities into your life: focus on a hobby, spend time with family, or simply take time to be present in the moment. Find the right balance for you and make it a non-negotiable requirement in your life.

WHAT YOU NEED TO KNOW

Strong leaders develop and sustain healthy boundaries. Remember to establish and incorporate your preferred personal and professional balance in an effort to avoid burnout.

The following skills can help as you continue to define your desired boundaries in the workplace:

SKILLS	
	Find the balance.
	Self-care is a requirement.
	"No" is a full sentence.

The reflective prompts shared throughout this chapter are designed to help you consider your purpose and expectations that you are hoping to achieve as you intentionally utilize these techniques.

FIND THE BALANCE. While what constitutes work and life balance looks different for everyone, typically responsibilities increase as you grow older. As such, it is easy to get consumed in the act of "doing" and not living fully. Identify a work-life rhythm that protects your core identity. Finding the balance is the act of choosing to provide for others with the caveat that you reserve fuel in your tank to uplift and care for yourself. You are accountable for ensuring that you find happiness and fulfillment in your life. You know best how to define work-life balance on your terms.

* How do you define work and life balance?
* How can you protect your requirements while supporting the needs of others?

* Why is it important to take accountability for establishing personal boundaries?

SELF-CARE IS A REQUIREMENT. Sometimes you need a gentle reminder to love on yourself. You may feel selfish if you prioritize your needs over those of others, but you have a responsibility and duty to preserve the time for yourself. Self-care is a requirement in both professional and personal settings. You are in charge of monitoring the level of fuel in your tank and need to stop for refueling. Take the time to make sure you have what you need to sustain your pace. This will help you show up in a positive way at work and for your loved ones.

* What is something that you do weekly that is just for your personal enjoyment?
* How can you carve out time to do something that you want to do (regardless of importance)?
* What will happen if you constantly pour from your bucket into other buckets without refilling your own?

"NO" IS A FULL SENTENCE. Saying "no" comes easily to some, and with apprehension or anxiety for others. You do enough for others at work and in your personal life. You get to decide when you need to take a break or step away from recurring activities. Leaders are have intense pressure to satisfy the needs of other people: our bosses, colleagues, peers, friends, family, neighbors, and the others who may come to you asking for your time. Add the sentence: 'No.' to your lexicon and feel proud of your ability to protect your sanity, health, and peace.

* How does the thought of disappointing someone that you care about make you feel?
* How often do you say 'yes,' when you want to say 'no'?
* What is one thing that you will say 'no' to in the next 30 days?

FINAL REFLECTION

* On a scale of 1 (poor) to 10 (superpower), how would you rate your ability to establish a work and life balance?
* What challenges have you faced when saying "no" to others?
* What opportunities may be present for you to consider after reading this chapter?

IN SUMMARY

EXHALE MORE THAN YOU INHALE. Choose to *find the balance, self-care is a requirement,* and *use no as a sentence.* This will ensure that you have the endurance to meet your broader objectives and can sustain your leadership power.

AFTERWORD

*"Give yourself grace, believe in your power
and move with purpose"*
-Dr. Monique Dawkins

Congratulations for sticking with it and making it to the end of these reflections and exercises aimed to help you build influence and elevate your leadership power. As you can see from Madison's story, some leadership paths can be compared to a roller-coaster ride. Along with thrilling highs and unexpected lows, and lots of twists and turns!

I hope you have taken some time to reflect on how you can practically apply the rules and skills shared in an impactful way that benefits you. Most important, I hope you realize that you are not the only one who goes through crazy experiences in the world of leadership. If you intentionally apply the lessons in this book, you will have the upper hand! You are a force with the talents, tools, and abilities that you can use to help yourself survive and thrive as a leader.

Acquiring the leadership title is the easy part! It takes time and practice to find the right balance of influence and power while maintaining your leadership integrity. When you demonstrate authentic leadership in a way that makes you feel good, you may receive praise from other leaders and feel energized. Despite experiencing a range of emotions along the way due to good, bad, and ugly experiences, you are still standing!

Celebrate the fact that you are stronger, wiser, and more intentional now that you have seen some things. You may not look like what you have been through, and it speaks volumes that you still choose to remain in leadership. Although you are not perfect, you are complete.

The rules of the workplace are plentiful and the manual on 'what to expect while leading with other leaders' is outdated and missing a few chapters. The unspoken rules, dirty rules, rules of thumb and ultimate rule are just a few that I deem important and have shared in this book. There are plenty of others. Be encouraged and know that you can overcome any challenge that presents itself along your professional journey. Believe in yourself and give yourself the permission to regularly showcase your talents and abilities.

My hope is that the rules shared in this book will help you to shape your perspective, provide fresh approaches and inspiration for you on your leadership journey. I hope that you feel inspired, confident, and ready to take action on your own terms!

ACKNOWLEDGEMENTS

First and foremost, I want to extend a thank you to my village. I am blessed and highly favored, and I have an abundance of friends, family, colleagues, clients, and supporters that root for my success. I am humbled by the love and support that I received during the writing process of this book. God continues to guide me, and I am choosing to follow my passion.

I want to start off by thanking my dream team! A huge thank you to my husband, Patrick for being my Chief of Everything (COE); without your encouragement, guidance and technical ability, this book would not exist. A special shout out to my editors, Nina, and Amanda; thank you for your insights and contribution to the manuscript. Thank you to my feedback team, Janelle, Lynda, Jeri and Carol for your eagle eyes and helpful suggestions. I am grateful for my heartbeats, Bryson and Mackenzie that remain patient and kind enough to share their mommy-time so that I could craft and curate this book.

I am known for encouraging others to dig deep and to 'do it anyway!' I had a message on my heart that developed over the twenty years of my professional career. I longed to contribute to the leadership self-help genre in a profound way. Instead of doubting myself, I went for it! I hope that you find inspiration and motivation to build influence and power in the way that suits you because-*You Know Best.*

ABOUT THE AUTHOR

Monique Dawkins, EdD, is a learning and organizational development thought leader, author, and executive coach. She holds a doctorate in Organizational Leadership and Adult Education from Columbia University and is known as a leading authority in workplace learning and talent management.

With over 20 years of experience in management roles, she brings extensive expertise in operational leadership, human resources, and change management. She has effectively coached hundreds of individuals—ranging from aspiring managers to C-suite level executive leaders. She is passionate about promoting authentic and transparent leadership principles to develop leaders and high-functioning teams.

Dr. Dawkins completed her undergraduate degree at Howard University and received a master's degree from Pace University. She holds Associate Coaching Certification from the International Coaching Federation (ICF) and a Strengths Coaching Certification from Gallup.

LEARN MORE

Please Be Kind and Leave a Review
(Amazon, Barnes and Noble or Good Reads)

Book Discussion Guide and More
www.moniquedawkins.com

Coaching, Consulting and Training Info
www.betterequippedsolutions.com

CPSIA information can be obtained
at www.ICGtesting.com
Printed in the USA
BVHW042003130423
662303BV00003B/9